SHE LEADS FROM WITHIN

Intuitive Thought Leadership is
Changing the Way Women Do
Business

SHE LEADS FROM

WITHIN

Intuitive Thought Leadership is
Changing the Way Women Do
Business

For permission requests, write to the publisher at the address below.

E.P. House
www.ephouse.co

This is a work of nonfiction. Nonetheless, some names, identifying details and personal characteristics of the individuals involved have been changed. In addition, certain people who appear in these pages are composites of a number of individuals and their experiences.

The views and ideas expressed in this book are those of the author and do not reflect those of E.P. House.

Library of Congress Cataloging-in-Publication Data is available.

First paperback edition - May 2024
Paperback ISBN: 979-8-8693-3269-1
Digital ISBN: 979-8-8693-3270-7

PRINTED IN THE UNITED STATES OF AMERICA ON ACID-FREE PAPER

Cover Design by Taylor Lisney

Proceeds of this book go to support Women
United, a nonprofit that empowers
women globally by fostering leadership,
advocacy and positive change.

Your contribution helps us uplift women
everywhere.

···· TABLE OF CONTENTS

15

1 ⋯ AWAKENING MY FEMININE POWER

by Wonderful Morrison

I am the great-great-granddaughter of Segundina Famor Remotigue, I am the great-granddaughter of Catalina Remotigue, I am the granddaughter of Felisa Remotigue Palabrica, and I am the daughter of Almalita Palabrica Biugos. I have the knowledge of four generations of women on my maternal side, they represent the path to the awakened feminine power that is mine to possess. But ... what does that mean? Why does it matter? How does this affect me now? And how does it affect my daughters and granddaughters?

Almost eight years ago, I was at a ranch in northern California embarking on a journey of personal development for women leaders.

This was an experience I was ecstatic about, and yet terrified.

What?

I paid five thousand dollars for something I would never do, given a choice. I thought I had signed up for a seminar style retreat experience where we would sing around the campfire, sleep indoors, and have chefs cooking up our meals while professional facilitators led us. Well, I *did* sign up for that, but it also came with an outdoor experience, a group community project—like habitat for humanity—rock climbing and zipline (I gotta get better at reading the fine print!). While reading the email, I knew I had a choice. I could email them back to say that I had changed my mind, ask for a refund, and go on with my life. *Or* go for it, surrender to my fear, and see what would happen. I mean, what is personal development if I didn't choose brave, So I gathered everything on that list and *off I went*!

The word "powerless" is the ugliest word in the English language, it evokes in me the feeling of a cement block tied to my ankle pulling me down to the bottom of the ocean. I can feel the tightness of my chest, suffocating the breath within me, dragging me into the darkness of the ocean depth. A place where I am at the bottom of the food chain, a place where silence is in its constant state, a place where things and people are forgotten, because it is the place where anything that wasn't originally there can exist.

It is the *void* of human existence.

At a very young age I understood what being powerless meant. My father had subscribed to disciplining children with an iron rod—sometimes literally—when his anger flared, which was often triggered by a tiny speck of dirt on my dress to not making my bed properly. He would go into a rage, explaining that it came from his love for us. His choice of apparatus for punishment was whatever object was in close proximity. Due to these types of unpredictable violent outbursts, I quickly acclimated and forged an internal world of survival. I studied, observed, mimicked and adjusted once I mastered that I developed my version of "power." My resilience, grit and fortitude were born out of anger, the anger that continuously grew inside me from being treated like a caged animal. This quickly taught me a very important survival skill, *do not* put yourself in environments you cannot *control*.

I thought I must have been a glutton for punishment, why would I willingly pay for an experience that literally put me in a position that was opposite of having control?

There is a Native American legend that tells a tale of an old Cherokee teaching his grandson about life.

"A fight is going on inside me," he said to the boy. "It is a terrible fight, and it is between two wolves. One is evil—he is anger, envy, sorrow, regret, greed, arrogance, self-pity, guilt, resentment, inferiority, lies, false pride, superiority, and ego."

He continued, "The other is good—he is joy, peace, love, hope, serenity, humility, kindness, benevolence, empathy, generosity, truth, compassion, and faith. The same fight is going on inside you – and inside every other person, too."

The grandson thought about it for a minute and then asked his grandfather, "Which wolf will win?"

The old Cherokee simply replied, "The one you feed."

The moment finally arrived; it was time for the overnight "solo" camping event. Until that moment I had never camped outdoors, pitched a tent, or had a single desire to do anything close. I was not emotionally prepared. We were dispersed in groups of ten at different locations throughout the sprawling two thousand acres of land. We were all between forty to a hundred feet apart, far enough that we were on our own but close enough to find each other if danger arose.

I felt like a fish out of water, my anxiety was on high alert, as I looked around, I realized we were nowhere near the main campus or a road of any kind, just surrounded by mountain ranges as far as the eye could see. The facilitators suggested taking advantage of the quiet time around nature to "write in our journals, meditate, be still and with ourselves." Suggestions that in all honesty were unfamiliar to me. As a young mom with three kids, my alone time was mostly hiding in the bathroom. Not knowing what to do in an environment that was about me with no one around to talk to was skin-crawling uncomfortable. I sat on the ground looking at my unpitched tent that I had no clue how to even begin putting together, my backpack wasn't even worth unpacking because … well, how would I put it all back together again? Feeling a sense of hopelessness, I started to cry. I wanted to get on the walkie talkie, tell them to come get me and take me back to the main campus so I could call my husband and have him fly out from Seattle to California to come get me.

Why did I sign up for this? I asked myself. *What growth did I need from this? What is the purpose of being here if being uncomfortable was the thing that would break me? If growing up with a violent hostile father was not going to break me, how was camping solo the thing that would do me in?*

As this final thought crossed my mind I shot up, faced the sun, closed my eyes, and focused on my breath over and over again until I could feel the calmness penetrating throughout my body. When I opened my eyes again, I had a renewed fervor to face my demons. I picked up my tent bag, read the instructions and went for it.

French Poet Jean De La Fontaine once said, "A person often meets his destiny on the road he took to avoid it."

When the sun went down and the night's darkness covered the sky, I hit a new level of uncertain chaos. My nervous system became completely unhinged. My mind wandered into the abyss of "what ifs." What if a bear decided to claw me to death or a mountain lion who hadn't eaten in days came across my campsite and ate me for dinner? Or, what if I had to pee or go number two? I don't have the strength to hold it all night. And who knew what was lurking on the ground, or in the trees!

As my anxiety headed into overdrive, my survival brain kicked in and I refocused my mind by looking up at the star-filled sky; my breath started to slow and my body started to relax. I recognized the magnitude of this experience. I remembered reading once that inside each one of us are the same elements of stardust that are in every star in the sky. *How dare I dim that light*, I thought. I wrapped myself in my blanket and started counting the stars until I eventually fell asleep.

The howling of the wind woke me up. I was startled by its strength. It shook my tent, which wasn't what scared me. What truly scared me was the turbulent anger of the wind. Its roar made me feel insignificant and small; easy to throw around. Panic set in, my body started to rattle, my teeth began to chatter, and I couldn't understand what was happening. It wasn't freezing. Why was my body reacting like I was in the middle of a snowstorm in my underwear? I felt like a scared 7-year-old waiting for my father's wrath. I could feel tears welling up. My throat tightened and my thoughts whirling deeper into an unknown cave of darkness. So, I did what I had done as a child when scared out of my mind, I squeezed my eyes shut. If I couldn't see the monster that might appear, I could convince myself my fear was not real. My jaw clenched, my body tensed, my knuckles whitened as I held my blanket with a death grip. Then suddenly, there was silence, the air stood calm. *Had I been transported elsewhere? Did I just teleport?*

My teeth stopped chattering, my body slowly unclenched, there was a warmth in the air that embraced me. I slowly opened one eye to see if I was still in my tent and scanned the space, when I saw something or someone sitting at the corner of my tent. I couldn't make out who or what it was. I opened my other eye to have a full view of what I thought was my imagination, and there she was. My grandmother, Felisa. We had never met in person, but I knew who she was immediately. She smiled at me, her eyes soft and her gaze loving. I did not move, I thought I must be hallucinating. *Did I accidentally eat a wild mushroom earlier that day? I did see one next to my campsite, right?* Then, she opened her mouth, and spoke. Her voice was weirdly familiar. It was eerie and comforting.

"Do not be afraid, I am here to tell you something," she said.

Still, I did not move a single inch of my body—not a micro movement of my eyes, not a blink.

"I want you to know that you come from a long line of powerful, strong women. There is nothing you cannot handle. We are a part of you, you are a part of us. You are the legacy of all those before you and all those who will come after you."

I sat up, tears streamed down my face. I had felt so alone since my mother's death, it had been twelve years without her guidance, without her comforting voice, without her love and care. My grandmother's words hit me at my core. I could see the strength in her eyes, I could feel her enormous energy of love. I knew in my heart that she saw me. She understood what I was seeking—the search for who I am, who I needed to be and who I wanted to become. She understood my pain and her presence comforted me. My eyes fixed on her. I wanted to move and hug her, but I couldn't. I wanted to speak, but I couldn't. There was so much I wanted to say, and yet no sound came out of my mouth. Her eyes spoke to me but I didn't understand. She smiled a warm smile, a gust of wind shook the tent and she was gone.

Till this day, I cannot fully comprehend what happened that night. What I do know is that her words are forever etched in my heart. The next morning, I didn't know what to do with the mystery of the evening so I told no one.

As the last days of the retreat were coming to an end, I had found a new version of me on that ranch. Every day was uncomfortable and unpleasant. They challenged me, called me out, tore down my walls, and tested my beliefs. I had a love/hate relationship with it; it wasn't what I had expected but was exactly what I needed. The day came and it was time to go back to our lives, our families, our situations, and to live out our renewed selves. We loaded the bus but the air felt different somehow that time, like we were a new group of women—a little bit stronger, a little bit lighter, a little bit more of our true selves. There was a lot of chatter, laughter and love. You could feel the energetic vibration at its highest peak as we settled into our seats. We had each arrived nine days prior from different spaces in our lives—some good, some great, some bad, some stuck—but that day we found ourselves leaving happier, open and ready for what was ahead. Driving away I looked back from the rear window of the bus sending the ranch my love and gratitude, bowing to its power to break us open and gifting us with the truth. I said a little prayer and asked the spirit to give me strength to live the life I was meant to live, and I blew a kiss.

Four months later, my life imploded at DEFCON 1, the highest level of imminent danger urgent alert. My health, my business, my finances, my reputation, my family, and every other inch of my life took a tragic turn. I had been betrayed—betrayed *big* by people I loved and cared for deeply. My heartbreak was life-altering, the kind that only had two outcomes: death or life. And it ended up being the very thing that unleashed my feminine power, I just didn't know it at the time. As the days, months and years following started to unravel, the question I had to ask myself was which of the two wolves was I going to feed?

I look back on that night at the solo camping event; the way it tested my deepest fear of being out alone in the wild and I see that it was preparing me for what was to come soon afterwards. But most importantly, my grandmother's presence—my sage—came to me that night to inspire in me the courage to choose in feeding the good wolf. To choose joy, peace, love, hope, serenity, humility, kindness, empathy, generosity, truth, compassion and faith. In the aftermath of the tragic turn of events in my life that would last seven years, we lost everything we had worked for and had to rebuild from ground zero. That experience is not for the faint of heart.

Many times, in those seven years it would have been easier—even more comfortable—to have chosen rage, anger, violence and vengeance. I knew at the core of my being, at the very soul of who I am, that I couldn't be the example of self-worth and self-love to my children or my granddaughters from a place of fear. The rub is that all my life I have known only the opposite: how to survive in constant fear and my lifetime membership of compromising my emotional and physical safety to belong. You see, the biggest betrayal didn't come from other people, it came from within me. I have betrayed myself more than anyone else. When my grandmother told me that I come from a long line of strong and powerful women, what she was trying to tell me is to understand that I came from a family line of love and gratitude.

I didn't see it then but when I started to connect the dots of my family legacy, it was written in compassion and generosity that stems from the practice of forgiveness. The stories of my grandmother's heartache, lying on her death bed without her only daughter at her side, wasn't told from anger. It was told from a voice of hope and understanding. The story of my grandfather giving all his retirement money to his son-in-law—in hopes he would build a life for his daughter—only for the son-in-law to gamble it all away, was not told from disappointment or ego. It was told from the voice of empathy.

These are the kinds of stories embedded in the fabric of my family history. There are countless examples of hurt, pain and betrayal, yet none are told from a place of sorrow or regret. The stories are passed down generation after generation from the voice of love, faith, generosity and truth. I have found that it is impossible to live fully in gratitude and unconditional love without forgiveness. My journey of forgiveness has not been easy, but it has taught me to trust my own heart. It shows me that I am enough just as I am, and it has allowed me to accept my true worth.

It's fascinating to me that gratitude intuitively seeks forgiveness, and its reward is love. So, then what keeps us from doing it? What keeps us from forgiving? Why did it take me until I was broken to pursue forgiveness's healing power? I don't know the answer to these questions. What I do know is who I am today, who I am becoming, and who I want to be because of it.

Who am I today?

I am worthy simply because I am. I am love without judgment or condition. I am a creative genius. I am an unwavering support to those around me. I am courageous and I am in love with myself.

Who am I becoming?

I am becoming a more powerful version of myself every day. I am becoming aligned with my heart, body and soul. I am becoming the storyteller I was meant to be. I am becoming my authentic self, more and more each day.

Who do I want to become?

I want to become a mother and grandmother who embodies forgiveness. I want to become a woman who exudes strength in the face of adversity. I want to become someone whose love fills every empty cup of the women who go behind me.

I no longer carry my shame as a badge of honor, nor do I wear my armor to hide my vulnerability. I have retired my sword that cuts things down and could potentially hurt me. I no longer have the urge to run away from things that might be scary. I feel my feelings no matter how hard. I have outgrown self-punishment. I respect my thoughts and ideas no matter how silly they might be. I honor all parts of me. I am kind and gentle with myself when facing the unknown. I love myself unconditionally.

We all have the power to choose who we feed. Will it be the good wolf, or will it be the bad wolf?

I am the great-great-granddaughter of Segundina Famor Remotigue. I am the great-granddaughter of Catalina Remotigue. I am the granddaughter of Felisa Remotigue Palabrica. And I am the daughter of Almalita Palabrica Biugos. I come from a long line of powerful and strong women. I now represent the path to the awakened feminine power, and it is mine to possess.

What about *you*?

··· ABOUT WONDERFUL MORRISON

Wonderful Morrison isn't just your average CEO – she's a fiery champion on a mission to empower high-achieving women entrepreneurs. As the driving force behind Leadher Brand & Marketing Consulting Agency, she's fueled by a burning passion to catalyze transformation and empowerment. With over 25 years of entrepreneurial experience under her belt, Wonderful has witnessed firsthand the incredible power of strategic branding and marketing. At Leadher, each and every strategy is infused with her unwavering passion and determination, igniting the flames of success for her clients. She firmly believes in the awe-inspiring synergy that occurs when evolution meets alignment, which is why Leadher's couture branding and marketing solutions are meticulously crafted to reflect the essence of each client, amplify their unique voice, and deeply resonate with their audience. Together, with her clients, Wonderful is committed to igniting the flames of evolution and soaring to new heights of success and fulfillment. But her passion doesn't end there. Beyond her entrepreneurial pursuits, Wonderful finds boundless joy in her role as a mother to three remarkable grown children and a grandmother to two lovely granddaughters. Her journey began when she met her husband at the age of nineteen, and she cherishes waking up to him each morning. Join Wonderful on this extraordinary journey as she champions fempreneurs everywhere, redefining the landscape of success with her unstoppable passion and drive. Together, let's make waves and leave an indelible mark on the world.

Facebook: *https://www.facebook.com/morrisonwonderful*
Facebook Private Group Page: *https://www.facebook.com/groups/leadhercommunity*
Facebook Business Page: *https://www.facebook.com/leadherbizacademy*
Instagram: *https://www.instagram.com/wonderful_morrison*
LinkedIn: *https://www.linkedin.com/in/wonderfulmorrison*

2 ··· RACEHORSE TO GRACE HORSE

by Sandy Stamato

What do a traumatic brain injury, hyper-achiever sales extraordinaire and cancer have in common? Me. And what does this have to do with the topic of this book? Everything.

"Get Sandy to do it. She's a machine! That girl is unstoppable."

I've heard a variation of this my whole work life. Whether selling advertising, being director of business development for a creative agency, a corporate trainer for sales representatives and entrepreneurs, or building my own consulting business, I always put 100% of myself into everything

I did. Once I connected with the vision and mission of whatever I was selling, the click happened, and I was off to the race. Every so often, though, I'd hear a little voice in my head saying, *"What race am I in? Is there a finish line? What am I doing?"*

At fifty-two years old, I was at the top of my game, and I was rockin' it. I was the #1 salesperson at the organization I worked for, meeting and presenting to major ad agencies, and frequently, a keynote speaker at large events. There was even time for a seat on a couple of boards of directors. I was doing what I loved. I represented an organization whose vision and mission I adored. I got accolades, prizes, and bonuses. I hit all my financial goals and usually exceeded them. I recollect being complimented or praised for my accomplishments, to which I'd murmur a comment, "Oh, I was just lucky," not wanting to appear like a "tall poppy," as my Australian buddy calls it, or "too big for my britches," a refrain I frequently heard from my grandmother.

I wasn't lucky. I worked my ass off for everything I did. This was nothing new. I was usually one of the top salespersons wherever I worked. I have a gift for sales. I loved the whole process: meeting with new people, finding out what they need, and then offering them a solution. I met some great people and built lovely relationships with my clients.

Yet, the challenge with straight commission sales and entrepreneurship is this reality: No sales, no money in the bank. No money in the bank, no mortgage payment. So, the minute my alarm went off, this insistent inner voice started chanting, *"GO! Money is time. Time is money."* This fueled my internal drive. However, I was in a constant internal struggle between trusting myself/intuition and the Universe and "go!" Sadly, "go" won out many times. I couldn't fathom how to operate any differently. I had a spiritual practice, a community, a husband, and friends. I knew that Spirit/God/Buddha truly had my back. To a certain degree. But I didn't believe it one hundred percent.

The Silent Driver

I heard someone say once, "It's what we don't know about ourselves that runs us."

And fear was running my show.

It was the waters I swam in.

My amazing husband would wait at home for me with dinner on the stove, and I'd call and say, "I'll be home in fifteen minutes," which meant at least an hour or two.

When he got upset, I'd think to myself, *He doesn't understand! I am the major breadwinner. I had proposals to write, client meetings, emails, presentations to create, orders to be placed, etc., and that took time.* Truth be told, what I really thought was, "You don't understand how important this is. Okay, how important I *am*. I'm bringing home big bucks, so back off," Of course, he didn't understand. He just wanted to see his wife.

I just didn't know how to turn it off.

Remember—Time is money. Money is time.

Salespeople and entrepreneurs are a different breed of cat. We thrive on the drama and challenge of it all. I know I did. The problem was, I wasn't paying attention to the rest of my life. I gave up drinking when I was twenty-five (or someone might say that drinking gave up on me!), but that's a different story. I just transferred all that itch and addictive behavior to my work. I didn't have a stop button. Even though, I was receiving signs from the Universe to do just that.

I was rear-ended at least four times in seven years, and not once was I at fault. I recall a couple of folks saying that this might be a little sign to slow down. I thanked them for their profound insight and zipped right back into my life. My deepest desire, however, was to have a balanced life. If I could just be balanced, I could relax. When I eventually left my sales job, I thought, *"Now is the time to create this elusive balance."*

That following weekend, I developed two websites: one for my blossoming jewelry design biz, which I had been doing on the side (oh, did I forget to mention my side hustles?) and was very popular. The other was my consulting business supporting female entrepreneurs challenged with "selling" themselves and their services.

See? Balanced.

Okay, maybe I spent more time making jewelry for upcoming shows than I ever did at my previous job. Or spent most of my days networking and meeting people, promoting my consulting business? This was balance, as far as I knew. And I enjoyed it. The Monday after I launched my two websites, I got rear-ended. *Again.*

Seriously, Universe. Wtf?

This one was a little different, from the others because I felt really off and mentally slow. *Nothing a bit of coffee can't fix, right?* My doctor was concerned. I agreed and did what I knew to do—I went right back to it. Then, one day, boom, it all stopped … dramatically, catastrophically, and in my deepest fear, irreparable.

I remember it was a sunny Seattle day. I was going to visit my sister. It was rush hour, and for a change, I was on time and even doing the speed limit—rare. I stopped at a red light, and a young kid behind me was texting, didn't see the light, and plowed right into my car going thirty-five miles an hour.

The sound of metal hitting metal enveloped me.

Time slowed down to an eerie crawl. I felt a slow, relentless wave of force that surged through the vehicle until it struck me like an immovable weight, slamming my body into the wheel and then snapping my head against the headrest with deadly precision. I was plunged into a world where time stood still. Everything stopped. Traffic was backed up. People were screaming. Someone yelled, "Call an ambulance!" I wasn't bleeding so, I waved her off. Yet, off to the hospital I went anyway. The ER said nothing was broken and sent me home. (I should have had frequent flyer miles by then.)

Thus began a terrifying and horrific period before I was diagnosed. I looked okay but felt like I was adrift in no man's land. I would scream at my husband, hang up on my mother, and rage at my beloved mentor and sponsor, who had been in my life for twenty-five years.

For that first month, my new mantra was, "What's wrong with you? Get up and move, your lazy ass." My constant self-deprecation was accompanied by a sense of flatness and frequented by uncontrollable bursts of rage and tears. I had been a member of a big networking group that met weekly. I was trying to act like things were "fine." Each week, we stood up and gave our forty-five-second commercial. It would take me two hours, lots of tears, and anxiety to try and memorize something that I historically could ad-lib with ease. I was mortified and didn't know what was happening to me.

My sister suggested I get a lawyer. I'd shut her down, but she persisted. Finally, she got through. She connected me with Roxanne, whom I'd coincidentally met years before she started practicing law. After hugs and "small world" chit-chat, I tried to explain what happened, and before I got halfway through, she interrupted with, "Sandy, I need you to hear me. You aren't the same. Something's going on. And I want you to get tested for a traumatic brain injury—a TBI" I burst into tears, mostly from relief. At least now I had a name for what I was feeling. And thus started my journey into the world of rehabilitation and cognitive tests that left me fearful and exhausted.

Here's the bitch about a TBI: it's called the invisible wound. I looked normal. Granted, it was a banner day when I showered, and for some reason, I wore the same pair of pants everywhere. I just couldn't fathom making fashion choices; it felt overwhelming. My husband made sure they were washed.

Frankly, I didn't care.

The best way I can describe what a TBI feels like is this. Imagine you want to drive home. You know where you want to go and you've gone the same route thousands of times, but now you can't figure out how to do it. You're lost.

It's terrifying.

To address my emotional and mental issues, I joined a support group and connected with other invisible wounded "TBIers." I worked with an amazing neurologist, a TBI therapist, and a speech pathologist at the University of Washington Hospital. I slowly learned how to work with my brain in a completely new way.

I began to know how to schedule my days. I designed jewelry, which I had a flair for, but I gave up on consulting. I took workshops and participated in any offering for TBI folks. I was doing all the right stuff, but I was still feeling so lost. I just wanted to get better.

Neuroplasticity was not as widely acknowledged as it is now. At the time, conventional wisdom said that wherever you were cognitively at the two-year mark, that's as far as your brain could heal. Thank God, my neurologist didn't believe that and said that our brains continue to heal and change. He explained about neuroplasticity, and I held onto that.

I had been a very successful, over-achiever with a fantastic track record, who was terrified to get a part-time job at a bead store because I didn't think I was smart enough to work the register.

I was put on anxiety medication and began taking naps. I learned all about neuro-fatigue and that my brain got fuzzy after a certain amount of time. I started receiving disability, which helped tremendously with the mounting bills. I hung out with some people whose identity revolved around the words, "I am disabled." I didn't want that, but I was just so grateful that they let me hang with them.

About two years into my rehab, my speech pathologist invited all her patients to a special event. There were about eight of us in this group. A meditation teacher was going to lead us into a deep contemplation and meditative process.

I was thrilled! *Sign me up!* In the past, I participated in Vipassana/Insight meditation. I'd attended several silent retreats for 3 to 10 days at a time. *"Finally,"* I thought to myself, *"I got this! I'll show my fellow TBI-ers how it's done. I'm going to ace this."*

But the strangest thing happened when I arrived at the event. It was a typical overcast, gray day in Seattle. I was running late. As I parked my car and started walking toward the building, I began feeling a little anxious. I kept telling myself, *"Knock it off; this is your thing. Chill."* But I couldn't.

As I entered the lobby, I noticed with each step that my anxiety notched up the closer I got to the conference room. The same room where I had taken many classes. I didn't get it. I loved meditation in the past. Granted, I hadn't done a Vipassana retreat in a long time, but I cherished the times I did. I "met myself" during a retreat. I had discovered a sanctuary within myself that was precious and sacred. It was my intuition, my true north, through thick and thin, I knew this was my Spirit. My safe place. I paused and entered.

Everybody was seated in a circle. I greeted folks and sat down, acting "normal." But internally, I was having a meltdown. I forced myself to breathe while listening to this lovely meditation teacher explain her process. She asked us to take some deep breaths and sink into our bodies. She asked us to gently close our eyes as she began the practice. I couldn't shut my eyes. I could barely breathe. I was terrified. She didn't notice at first, but when she saw me, she paused. She gently asked the group to open their eyes and come back together again.

Oh, her eyes. There was so much compassion and kindness as she looked at me and asked what was going on and if I wanted to share. I didn't know what to say when suddenly, the dam burst, and these words just spilled out from a place so deep inside that I couldn't hold back if I wanted to. "I'm terrified that if I close my eyes and tap into my Sacred Place, my Sanctuary, there won't be anything there. What if the car accident took that, too?"

She listened and gently said, "Honey, your place? Your Sacred Sanctuary? That's a place that neither trauma, car accidents, illness, or abuse can touch. It's untouchable. It's the essence of who you are, and it's eternal and sacred…nothing can touch it." And for the first time in two years, I heard my Sacred Sanctuary whisper, "Sweet one, it's going to be OK. You're going to be OK. Beyond what you can imagine. You're safe."

The Turning Point

I knew I was going to be okay.

It's been eleven years since the accident. It's been extraordinary. I went back to school and became a credentialed coach seven years ago. Then, recently I became a certified Positive Intelligence™ Coach. I love what I do. I work with female entrepreneurs and Positive Intelligence to help them with a Shame Free Approach to Sales. Cool, right? The first month I started this specialty, I tripled my income. I was *back*! I dove into my practice and that same cycle of working a lot. I said yes to all sorts of opportunities. I have a girl squad of fellow entrepreneurs that I adore and respect. I found my groove.

Then, I was diagnosed with breast cancer.

I spent the first couple of months in a fog. "Sandy" and "cancer" in the same sentence made no sense. It baffled me. It just didn't make sense. I couldn't concentrate on my business. I was busy getting tests, doctor appointments, and more tests. A lumpectomy changed to a mastectomy as the tests discovered more and more. I'm blessed that it was caught so early, as it was an aggressive type of cancer, yet very treatable. I've had incredible care. Yet, I grappled with thoughts of, *Am I being punished? Did my childhood, scary God, have it out for me? What did it all mean?*

I found my answer.

I was about a week after my mastectomy surgery. I woke up and instinctively placed my hand on my mastectomy site. For the first time since I was twelve years old, I could feel my actual heartbeat. It took my breath away. There was no barrier, no breast in the way. I felt *my heart*, the power and beat of this amazing organ. I started to cry. At that moment, in the stillness of the morning, I knew with certainty that my heart/my sanctuary didn't believe in punishment. I didn't know more than that, but it was enough. I heard a whisper *"Sweetie, you're never punished. You got cancer; that's all. You're going to be okay."*

With some trepidation, I decided to take a three-month medical leave once I found out that I needed chemotherapy. And, of course, I pushed back. That "drive" that kept me moving, thought it was a good idea to start a Positive Intelligence program during chemotherapy. *Easy peasy, right? What was I thinking?*

Luckily, I was able to listen to a dear friend who looked at me and said, "Sandy, why don't you just heal? This will be your full-time job. It's the kindest thing you can do for yourself."

I heard it.

Upon this decision and realization, and immediate sense of terror seized me. *What happens if people forget me? What if they stop inviting me to events that I'm always too sick to attend?* I took a deep breath and realized that *this* was the voice that wanted me to go, go, go. There is such freedom in self-awareness—thank you, Positive Intelligence. Thankfully, I have been able to shift away from those cruel thoughts. Instead, I am in a sense of wonder and curiosity about this next phase of my life. Don't get me wrong, chemo sucks. It does. I'm cancer-free, and the chemotherapy is preventative to ensure nothing snuck into my bloodstream. My hair is now falling out, and I'm sporting a new trendy buzz cut. My hair will grow back.

A New Quest

I'm having reconstructive surgery later in the year, where the flesh from my belly will create a new breast. But I can't take tissue from my belly—an area that I've loathed most of my life—and place that in my sweet breast site without exploring what self-love truly looks like for me. That's my new quest: to love myself. I've been given this incredible opportunity—a place to pause—a place to ponder the possibilities of what I want my life to look like and how I want to live it.

I do know my work life has to change. I love what I do and am called to do it. But not at the same pace I've worked at. I don't want to. I can't do that to my body or my spirit. I'm tired. I'm tired of this cycle of *work till I drop*. I want space in my days to "be." I get to create what my life looks like. This is what I desire.

Recently, I had tea with a neighbor whom I've known for seven years but never had a chance to talk with. She's lovely. I want more of *that*. I want to take more walks and connect with my women folk. I want to spend more time with my sisters and friends. I want to work with clients in small groups and at a pace that feels right to me. I want to write a book. I want to make some more jewelry. I want to road trip to Colorado to see friends with my sweetie, visit my in-laws in Florida, drive to the coast and feel ocean spray on my beautiful, bald head.

I don't know what the future will hold. But I do know that my Sacred Sanctuary loves me, and I get to discover what life could be and what I want it to be.

Stay tuned …

··· ABOUT SANDY STAMATO

This is Sandy's first foray into writing. She grew up with the belief that she didn't get the "writing" gene. Her sister got it. She didn't think she got the creativity gene, either (yup, another sister grabbed that one). So, imagine her surprise when at age fifty she took a jewelry class, loved it and has sold many of her designs. Take that "gene pool." Sandy started off her work career in TV—behind the camera. While working for ABC News, she had a eureka moment after reading a magazine article. A journalist was invited to write a story about a personal development retreat. The facilitator kept encouraging him to participate in the retreat to which he replied, "The job of a journalist is to simply observe." "That's IT." she proclaimed, "this is why I don't like TV. I want to participate." Thus began her 35-year career in sales, marketing and training. She loved her career. Why? Because it was all about connecting and relationships. She never felt like an observer again, she was fully participating. She worked with Ad Agencies, sold advertising, trained salespeople, consulted. She designed and created training programs on serious topics like "Conflict Resolution" only she made it fun. That was—and is—her secret sauce. Fun. The world is way too serious, and her guilty pleasure is finding those moments of levity to add a little funny/laugh. Sandy has always marched to the beat of a different drum. Her passion in life is to help others discover their own rhythm. As a "LimbDweller*" Coach for female Entrepreneurs, she creates a shame-free zone to learn how to sell. This radical approach to sales includes a dash of fun (of course!). She now spends her days, writing, working with clients, hanging with her NY hottie husband and doggie, Rio in Seattle Washington.

Facebook: *https://www.facebook.com/Limbdwellercoaching*
Instagram: *https://www.instagram.com/limbdwellercoaching*
LinkedIn: *https://www.linkedin.com/in/limbdwellercoaching*
Website*: https://www.limbdweller.com*
*What is a LimbDweller? *https://vimeo.com/manage/videos/500667219*

3 .... MYSTICAL MAGIC OF SAYING " YES"

by Sharon Maureen Hockenbury

It was my third birth of nine, and not "planned." I say that with tongue in cheek. There is a mystical working where our intuition, intention and soul's purpose align. Magic happens. It becomes part of the unplanned plan.

Preparing for admission to the hospital included several steps. First step, I signed some of the pre-op paperwork as it would be my third c-section. The admission clerk with her preppy efficiency slid it over.

"This is permission to do the c-section," she said. Signed.

"This is the paperwork for the tubal ligation—a permanent form of birth control."

As if in slow motion, the paper slid back towards me as I picked my pen back up. It seemed logical. I had a boy and a girl, and the doctors were going to be "in there anyway." I would not need an extra visit another time. At twenty-seven years old with soon-to-be three children, it seemed the "wise" choice. Right?

Ink in hand, I took the paper and felt this intense gripping in my gut. It was not pain but what felt like extreme hunger meshed with something from deep within my soul. I took a breath and checked in with myself. I knew my intuition was speaking, in fact screaming at me through my body.

Do not sign that paper!

I pushed the paper back to the receptionist saying, "I cannot sign this." She questioned my decision, but I knew my heart had spoken and my decision was firm.

The surgery was uneventful and my toe-headed bundle, Trey, was born. Nothing compares to embracing a newborn in your arms. Even though this was my third time around, it was as fresh, exciting, and intimate as my first. The nine-plus pound package of love I held in my arms would be a teacher of the most profound lessons. As I had done two times before, I snuggled him to my breast to give him the nourishment from my body. He latched and struggled. Not the normal, "I gotta figure this out" type of attempt, it was something more. Or so my heart said.

I attempted several more times. Finally, he began to draw richness from me. With relief, I smiled and held him close. The cherished moment was short-lived.

Again, something was not quite right, So, my heart said. I called for the nurse, asking for a pediatrician. Several hours later, after many more attempts to feed him, the doctor came to check him out. With bated breath, he delivered the news. Various syndromes rolled off his medically tamed tongue. All I could do was feel my heart sink.

"We are going to need to transport your baby to the Children's Hospital." I sobbed with a depth I did not know existed until that moment.

I experienced a roller coaster of emotions. It was beyond words, the height of hopefulness, the low of helplessness.

The next day I reunited with my baby in a lonely hospital room. Maneuvering the medical equipment, I could hold him, sing to him, and cuddle him. It brought comfort that a cold hospital bed could not. The luscious smell of a newborn is unmatched by even the most expensive perfume. The sterile smell that surrounded me could not smother his very essence. I inhaled deeply and prayed.

For the next seven weeks, the routine was the same, spending the early morning with my two little toddlers and then heading to the hospital. I spent the day hoping that my warm embrace would bring healing to this treasure I had formed in my womb. I would head home to my two children at night. Their sloppy kisses and sweet hugs brought strength to my weary body. I dropped into bed, exhausted in every sense of the word. Waking during the night, not to draw a warm baby to my breast but a cold hard phone to my ear. I dialed and, as always, a cheerful voice answered and put me on hold, listening to classical music while waiting for the nurse to come to answer my call. Receiving a report on how my son was doing, I got enough reassurance to drift back to sleep for a couple of hours. Jerking from a twilight slumber, I repeated the dialing mantra.

Each day, I arrived at the hospital to receive an update from the doctors. Enduring the report, my only goal was to hold my little guy as close for as long as I could without interruption. This was only a dream. The scurry of activity included pokes and prods and feeding through a tube. As he slipped off to a peaceful sleep, I would go to the pumping room and fill a bottle to the drone of a machine while my tears flowed.

Three weeks into this routine, an announcement finally came. A very technical surgical procedure would be the course of action. As Trey rolled down the ominous hall to the "prep" room, I said my goodbyes with a gentle kiss. The whoosh of the cold air from the surgery room doors brushed my face. A contrast against the warm tears that flowed once more.

It seemed hours before he returned to his room. The doctor gave a reassuring speech that all went well and as expected. I spent a few more hours whispering prayers and then headed home.

That evening, instead of dialing the phone when I awoke, a phone call startled me from a bone-weary sleep. The ring echoed at three in the morning, like a foghorn. It was the hospital.

"He has taken a turn for the worse. You need to come right away. We do not think he is going to make it."

I raced down a lonesome highway, desperate to save my baby. I wanted to keep him from leaving this earthy realm. Arriving at the hospital, my feet pattering the empty halls until I ran into my son's room. Filled with doctors trying to revive him, he laid bare and was fighting for his life. I lunged to his side and called his name, praying out loud.

And he began to teach his lesson.

He turned his little head tickled with strawberry blonde hair, toward me. A tear ran down his cheek. He seemed to be saying, "I am gonna give it all I've got." The tear-stained cheek spoke a lesson to my soul. The lesson was *hope.*

Do not lose hope!

Words echoed in my head. "Faith is the assurance of things hoped for," and, "there is no life without hope." We hope that all will be well and we hope for the best. We hope that there will be a way when there seems to be no way. And so, I began to speak words of faith, hope and love.

"You're gonna make it, little guy. Momma loves you so much. You can do it."

The breath of life filled his lungs and his heart began to beat. I saw a miracle performed in my midst. He was alive and I would continue to hope the best for him. He had suffered a stroke and the prognosis given by the doctors was not hopeful. Yet, my little teacher had taught me the importance of hope and I would not easily forget it.

He surpassed all expectations, as only we hoped he would. I remember the day he walked across the floor for the first time. I had hoped for that day, even though the prediction had been that day would never come. Hope gave us the endurance to persevere in seemingly hopeless circumstances. Hope inspired us to keep faith and hope did not disappoint us. Hope was the lesson channeled through a baby. I learned to keep my hope alive as I cared for this very special child. His care resulted in igniting my passion for health and wellness. As any mother would do, I took a deep dive to find out ways to support him and his unique needs. I became a certified herbalist and life coach, and have since helped hundreds of people take charge of their wellness and healing.

It can be challenging to accept that saying "yes" to our intuition does not always turn out the way we expect. Listening to intuition is about the moment. It is about universal energy, personal growth, and impact. Have you ever seen the Starlink in the sky? It is a cluster of individual satellites but from a distance it looks like a single strand. Every "yes" to our intuition may seem like an individual event, however, the beautiful string of yesses unite to sparkle like a streamlined Starlink.

When my intuition told me, "do not sign that paper," what was the result? Six more children! It is not what I predicted when I said "yes" to my intuition, but I do know it was right.

I had my fourth—a boy—who was born in the hospital without surgery. My next—a girl—was born at home. Number six began at home, but the birth ended up with a transport to the hospital after my uterus ruptured. I do not use the term lightly, but I experienced another miracle. Beating all odds, a healthy baby girl was born by surgery. At this point I am thinking, *what now?* "Your uterus cannot hold another pregnancy" was the declaration from the doctor. Back to my intuition and heart, and yes, I became pregnant with baby number seven.

By now, your mind might be whirling with thoughts. "This woman did *not* hear her intuition, she lost her mind."

I hear you, I had that thought myself. But there I was with another soul entrusted to me. I felt terrified and excited, I love being a mom. I loved nursing babies. I love the lessons I learned through my children. The skills I gained as a determined mother at home have served me well in my entrepreneurial journey. These skillsets have been instrumental in facilitating my service to my community. My faith and intuition fuel the calling I know I am destined for.

The seventh pregnancy was uneventful. Another surgical birth was scheduled due to the complications of the previous birth. The doctor was emphatic that the baby be born at least two weeks early. The days, weeks, and months rolled by as my belly rolled out. The beautiful autumn weather ensued and the scheduled due date was approaching. Then the unimaginable happened.

"Mommy, Mommy," I can't see!" The howl echoed through the hallway of our home. I stumbled my nine-month pregnant body out of bed, realizing the pressure of my bladder and the surge of fear. As I made my way down the hall, following the cries for help, my gut knew my life was about to change.

The extended family had gathered the night before. It was duck hunting season, and the fall tradition was in full swing. We were surrounded by aunts, uncles, first, second and third cousins and the merriment of gathering wafted throughout the house—laughter, memories, competition, comedic jabbing and mostly love. Trey had been enjoying the lively crowd. He announced that he wanted to name the soon-to-be-born baby "Tenille," even though we didn't know if it was a boy or a girl. His prophetic request became a namesake. Everyone had fallen into bed that night sleeping fitfully, anticipating the morning festivities. A cold October morning. Flannel and gloves. Hot chocolate in a thermos. A boat ride into the Puget Sound, a shotgun, the evening meal of duck mulligan stew.

It happened for years, serving generations. The men went out, mentoring the children in the art of patience and provision. The feathered prizes would soon be ready for the duck mulligan. The process included plucking the duck, except me. I broke tradition! When I got married part of our prenuptial agreement was, "no plucking duck!" I would cook but I would not pluck. I helped with home-baked sweets and savory dishes. All looked forward to the luscious dinner with the family gathered around the table. It did not happen for some.

I made my way that morning to Trey's bedroom. By then the household was bustling with worry. Trey was trying to find his way to the bathroom as his bodily functions dysfunction-ed. His head was pounding in pain, his eyes had lost their sight, and he stumbled along. A sense of terror was fully intact, mine and his.

"Mommy, Mommy, please … I can't see." He repeated again and again.

"It will be okay, honey. I love you. I love you." I held him in my arms, trying to bring comfort while my mind raced with the next step.

"Call 9-1-1!" I called out.

I placed Trey on the bed and proceeded to do what I had done hundreds of times before, offer comfort. I've never known such utter fright yet balanced with peace and strength. My husband had left before dawn for hunting. I sent word to the neighbors.

"Let him know he needs to hurry back."

He arrived as the ambulance screamed to the house.

The hospital room was cold … they always are. My body emerged in emotions and felt like an icebox. How can a room bustling with activity, nurses, doctors, aides, mom, and dad, seem so alone?

Once stabilized, Trey was airlifted to Children's Hospital. In his room, he seemed normal again. Though tired, he talked of his favorite baseball team and player. Then he said, "Let me sleep," and he did, peacefully. In a few hours, he was moved to another room. As I stood in the room, after a couple of medical procedures, I looked at the monitor Trey was hooked up to.

"Oh God, my God, his heart is slowing, no it is stopping!" I said in disbelief to the nurse.

The "flat line" alarm reverberated in the room and "code blue" echoed over the intercom. Every light in the room began to blink and then it became a mass of blue uniforms and my little-gowned boy.

He lay there motionless.

Years later the tears still flood my face. They flow and I remember. The blows to the chest and the resuscitation bag did nothing to call my little boy's soul back to his body. I stood at the precipice of life and death. Before me lay my ten-year-old son, lifeless, and I felt the baby in my womb meander and turn.

We made the choice.

The family stood around, along with some friends, and we faced the looming "pulling of the plug." We prayed for the resurrection of the dead. This miracle was not performed in our midst. We said our goodbyes and walked out of the room.

With an emptiness I had never known I had to make some challenging choices, which included postponing the scheduled birth. I needed to bury Trey. My body remained strong. How did I go on? The resilience of heart and mind, and the determination to take one step at a time and trusting the wisdom of divinely inspired heart. They are acts of faith, deep-seated love, and honor for the one who has departed. It is remembering that in the misery there is magic, as I had experienced many times before.

And you grieve.

Grief puts time at warp speed, but in slow motion.

It is a wisp.

The coffin was laid in the ground and balloons were symbolically released. The celebration of life, and then the birth of a baby girl one week later named "Tenille."

The grief process of years started. I had no regrets that I said "yes" to my intuition so many years ago. Tenille was a healing balm in the time of deep grief. I was strong amid the pain. Love carried me through trials. Rebound is possible, propelled by assurance in the cosmic purpose for my life from the cradle to the grave. A deeply held belief that all things work for good, even the bad is a hymn in my soul. Saying "yes" to my heart is always the best choice. I remember with thankfulness, Trey, a soul imparted to me for a short but impactful time. He taught me profound lessons and was an example of joy, fortitude, and moxie. And I grieved.

Grief is an energetic process, weaving to and through for the rest of our lives. It forces reflection where grace and compassion for yourself are vital. Many believe that we exist forever in some form. "Heaven," "walking streets of gold," "sitting at an eternal banquet table," "Nirvana," "to fully know and be fully known," and, "seeing Jesus' face," are a few of the descriptions, which in the end do not matter. In life, we need to embrace the process called life with a sense of surrender. In a full and fulfilling life there are tears, laughter, victory and defeat. We put trust in something "out there" that is written on all our hearts.

I listened to my intuition when Trey was born, many times before and so many times since. It is retrospection that has given me perspective. I will never regret saying yes to my intuition. The trials and the gifts are the essence of who I am and what I do. I went on to have two more children, after the death of Trey and the birth of his joyfully named sister, Tenille. For years, my life centered on the home. I continued to gain more knowledge and education about herbalism, health, and wellness. A passion unleashed out of painful circumstances blossomed into a beautiful outcome.

There was a health food store in my community that had been in existence for thirty-four years. My oldest daughter worked there as one of her first jobs. I frequented it often for my supplements and herbs, and to visit her. Always intrigued by the precious gem that served so many so well. It went on the market. I did not have *any* experience running a business. I was a domestic engineer with an entrepreneurial heart, and I could not let the niggle in my heart be ignored. I purchased the store and sought out educational opportunities to help me succeed. Business courses, finance courses, marketing courses and I was thriving. The compounding effect of saying "yes" to intuition is powerful. I am so thankful for the business I now run, the people I have been able to support, and the personal transformation I have experienced.

The mystery of intuition is indeed magical and practical. There is scientific research about the heart/gut/brain connection. Working with intuition is not about "making things happen." Aligning with a universal force from our intuitive souls will let things unfold with a sense of peace, yet it is not passive. It is a real and active part of our lives. We can choose to acknowledge it, work with it, and receive all the fullness of life that is possible. I have used this simple exercise with my life coaching clients to help them recognize and develop their intuition.

I encourage you to give it a try. Make a timeline of your life. Put things you remember and choices you made. Do not judge them as good or bad. Think about the times you chose from a deep place within you—your intuitive soul. Make a note and see how saying "yes" to your intuition weaved into something later on the timeline. What lessons did you learn? How has the lesson played out in your life? What impact for good did it have on others? This is how you will learn to listen to that still small voice inside.

One of the greatest mysteries of life is that of suffering, pain and sorrow. I do not pretend to understand. Listening to intuition is not about predicting outcomes. Listening to intuition is about faith and trust. It is about a life well lived, including grief and joy. It is sadness and happiness. It is about disappointment and deep satisfaction.

It is about being true to yourself.

··· ABOUT SHARON MAUREEN HOCKENBURY

Sharon Maureen Hockenbury is a multifaceted professional. She holds a Bachelor of Arts in Vocal Performance and is Certified as a Life Coach, Nutrition and Wellness Consultant, Herbalist, Reiki Master, Fitness instructor, and Hypnotherapist. She has supported 100s women through pregnancy and birth which was a source of deep satisfaction. She is the Creatrix of the Soulation Solution which empowers women in their third life chapter seeking more vitality, a deeper sense of purpose, and soulful alignment. Her Radio/Podcast "Soulation" is informative and inspirational. As a life coach, she offers innovative wisdom, powerful resourcefulness, and wit. She has spent several years adding to her skill set so she can offer the highest and best to her clients. As the owner of Twin Peaks Wellness Boutique, she has established herself as a cornerstone of her community, providing guidance, herbs, supplements, and healthy lifestyle choices. Sharon's passion for health and wellness was born out of experiencing and witnessing suffering. She set out on a journey to support her third child, Trey, who was born with a rare birth defect and then diagnosed with cancer at age 5. His tragic passing at 10.5 branded her heart to be a beacon of hope to those seeking answers for wellness in body, mind, and soul. Outside her professional life, she enjoys the outdoors including hiking and backpacking, creating fitness routines, singing and playing guitar, and hanging with friends. She deeply cherishes her family, including nine children, grandchildren, and her husband of over four decades, finding them to be her greatest teachers and source of inspiration.

Facebook: *https://www.facebook.com/houseful9*
Facebook Business Page: *https://www.facebook.com/twinpeaksnw*
Facebook: *https://www.facebook.com/sharonmaureenllc*
Website: *www.sharonmaureen.com*
Website: *www.twinpeaksnw.com*

4 ···· MIRRORS AND MAGNETS

by Brenda Reiss

I was drawn to Rob like a metal to magnet. Nothing could stop the attraction; I felt powerless to resist the pull. Our eyes met from across the room of a crowded event, and in an instant everyone and everything around me faded to a mistry gray. He was all I could see and finding my way across the room to him was all that mattered.

His charm was irresistible. His voice felt like breath. When he looked at me, I was certain that I saw my whole life mirrored in his eyes. Over the next months and years, I gave my whole self to creating a fairytale life, with his happiness at the center of it all. I believed I had found my dream-come-true life … but in reality, I nearly lost my soul.

My mirror of self-reflection was slowly shattered, and it would be a long, painful journey to finding my way back to my own heart.

Dear one, have you ever been charmed so completely by someone or something that you were willing to give up your whole self for it? Maybe it was a partner, or a business that didn't fit, or a life choice, or a belief that no longer served you? Have you ever experienced being held in a magnetic grip so powerful it caused you to surrender fully to another? If you have, then know that I am sharing my story for you. And it is my hope that my words help you find your way to a mirror that reflects to you the beauty of your own soul.

Although it would take a decade to release myself from his magnetic grip—and my own co-dependency—the fairytale began to shatter on our wedding day. After a whirlwind romance, I was to marry the man of my dreams. My heart soared, and my future was set. I planned to spend the rest of my life saying "yes" to my new husband's every wish.

On the way to the courthouse, tensions were high. Rob was distant and cold. I had never seen this side of him. When I asked what was wrong, we had our first argument. Something inside of me then whispered, "Brenda, this is not right. Don't do this." Desperate to keep the fairytale deception alive, I ignored Rob's troubling behavior and silenced those intuitive whispers. We married that day, and that night our shadow selves revealed themselves for the first time. His anger and emotional abuse met my co-dependency and desperate need for love and acceptance. We spent our wedding night in an ugly and hurtful fight.

Over the next decade together, we shared brief moments of bliss—just enough to keep me hooked into his magnetic force—but most days we brought out the worst in one another. Him: angry and controlling. Me: co-dependent and grasping for any sign of love. And yet, I still persisted, refusing to look into the mirror to see my soul fading away—bit by bit, day by day.

Sweet friend, if you've ever lived in this state, watching your soul-self hiding and/or fading away, then what came next for me might awaken something inside of you. Something that has been stirring for a very long time. Something good and true and worthy that wants to step out from the shadow and into the light.

It was the ninth year of our marriage that I started noticing a difference in his behavior. He became more distant, and I knew something wasn't right. Again, my intuition pinged, and I found myself wondering, "was there someone else?" When I asked, he told me "no," but the pinging only became louder. This time, I chose to listen to the intuitive whispers. I went looking for what I thought might be happening, and I found it. My heart plummeted. I was in shock; I couldn't breathe. Then the deep sobbing started. Instead of seeing who he was and what he was doing, I blamed myself.

What did I do wrong?

What could I have done differently?

Did I not matter to him at all?

I was desperate to get away from the pain and self-doubt and determined to escape the flawed woman I saw in the mirror. Not knowing where I was going, I got into my car. I needed to be anywhere but there. In that house. With that man. I found myself on a two-lane road in gut wrenching pain, tears streaming down my face. I couldn't figure out what to do with the pain. I couldn't be in it, and I didn't know how to escape it. It was then that I noticed the semi-truck ahead, driving towards me in the other lane.

In that moment, it just made sense. I gently guided my car into the trucker's lane. Heading straight for the oncoming truck, I knew it would only take a minute and the pain would stop. I closed my eyes, preparing for the end. Suddenly, something guided the steering wheel in the other direction, away from the truck. My hands were on the wheel, but I was not the one steering. As I slowed to a stop on the side of the road, not knowing what had happened, I felt tears subside as I heard the words.

"I got you."

Breathing in the moment, I had a deep knowing that I *did* matter and that I had some choices I needed to make. The magnetic bond with Rob had lost some of its strength and I began to catch a glimpse of my true self.

Sweet friend, I would love to report that I returned home and immediately began building a new life for myself. A life that reflected the truth of me. But no, big transformations are almost always messier than that. So, if you feel like your transformation isn't happening fast enough, keep going.

I returned home and tried to make the marriage work. I was determined to become the woman he could love. I became *more* attentive, *more* dutiful, and *more* determined to create the life I thought he wanted. I tried everything I could think of to fix the marriage—to fix me. But in the end, nothing worked. Rob didn't want to leave the affair.

This led to a year of deep reflection and self-discovery. We stayed in our home together, but we both knew the marriage was over. Finally accepting this, I devoted myself to healing my own traumatic wounds and freeing myself from the pull he had on me. I realized that I had an unhealthy addiction to being in love, so I entered a twelve-step program for sex and love addiction. I took classes and sought the help of healers, coaches and therapists. I took a deep and brutally honest look at my co-dependence and worked through my childhood beliefs that it was never safe to cause waves—because if I ever spoke up or caused even the tiniest wave in my family, I would get into trouble. And I wouldn't be loved.

It was slow and painful work, but in the end, I started to wake up to loving myself. My soul stepped forward and I embraced and embodied these truths:

- I matter.
- I can love myself.
- I deserve more than this.

I could finally see my true self reflected in the mirror. It was only then that I was able to release myself from the unrelenting magnetic pull the relationship with Rob had on me. I found myself standing in my kitchen giving my husband a choice—either we work on this relationship together and get the help we needed, or I needed to leave. It took every ounce of courage I had to be able to say that. I wanted him to say he would work to save our marriage.

"I can't do it, Brenda. I want to stay married, but I can't do what you are asking me to do," he said instead.

I paused and took a deep breath.

"Okay," I responded. "Then I need to leave."

Oh, sweet friend, this was the moment I finally took a step away from Rob and toward myself. If you've ever done the work to get to the other side of your pain and freed yourself to step forward and see your true self shining in the mirror, you will understand that this was one of those pivotal moments that changed the trajectory of my life. It is my hope that the six lessons I learned from this experience can serve as a mirror for you, helping you find your way to your own pivotal moments.

LESSON ONE—No one was coming to save me. I had to save myself. And, even harder than this, it was not my job to save anyone else.

Before the pivotal "kitchen encounter," I had spent my life giving away my power in relationships. I made the men in my life a priority over my own self, taking on their dreams and setting mine aside, not being able to set boundaries and stick up for myself, and not taking responsibility for my own thoughts and feelings. Being a "good" co-dependent, I worked tirelessly to not cause waves and focus my energy on making sure other's needs were met. It wasn't them doing that, it was *me*. I realized that I was the one responsible for my choices. And this woke me up.

It was up to me to make the changes I needed to make. There was no white knight coming to save me. It was up to *me*. Once I embraced this and began to live this new life, I saw that the opposite was also true. *It was not my job to save anyone else.* This allowed me to set Rob free to live his own life, learn his own lessons, and do his own healing work. Once I did this, the co-dependency began to loosen its grip.

LESSON TWO—Relationships are for growth and healing. They aren't "Hollywood fairytales." Instead, they are mirrors of *us*.

Relationships, whether romantic, personal or business-focused will always show us things about ourselves that we can't otherwise see. If you want to know what you dislike about yourself, simply look at what annoys you about the people who come into your life. Look into the mirror they provide. If you seem to attract angry people into your life, you may have some anger that you have not yet dealt with. If you find yourself surrounded by needy people, look for the neediness that lives within you.

LESSON THREE—Sometimes the mirrors offer a distorted reflection, so you must look with discernment.

If I focused exclusively on how and why Rob betrayed me, I was destined to stay stuck in anger and/or victimhood. But once I was willing to look at what else this reflection could be showing me, I was able to see it as a way to begin asking, "Where am I betraying *myself*?"

With that question in mind, the "mirror" showed me that by giving away my power, by not speaking up, and by putting my dreams on hold, I was betraying myself. Over and over and over again. I wasn't allowing myself to show up in the world and be the light that I came here to be.

By getting curious about *that* reflection, I was able to uncover parts of me that I had buried. This enabled me to start showing up and being present to life, knowing that my contribution matters.

LESSON FOUR—Control is an illusion.

When I looked at Rob's controlling behavior through a mirror of self-reflection, I saw my own desperate attempts to control my environment and the people around me. I discovered that the need to control was why I always strived to never cause waves. I believed that if I could keep everything under control then I could keep everyone happy. Then I would get what I needed, and *I would be safe.*

Control became a way for me to attempt to protect myself from the unknown. Some protective part inside of me believed that the more I could control the unknown, the less I would be hurt. But this was simply untrue.

Dear sweet one, here's the lesson within the lesson. Control is often an illusion, and almost always a futile and energy-wasting endeavor. Today, I am learning to have more trust in myself and that voice I heard in the car that day. Releasing the need to control and leaning into trust has enabled me to bring my power back to me, instead of continuing to give it away.

LESSON FIVE—Everything has purpose and meaning.

Think about it for a minute. Is there something that has happened in your life that felt so painful, or so challenging, that you didn't think you would ever be able to get through it? And later, were you able to see the blessing that came out of it? Maybe it brought about a solution or adventure you never thought possible. Or perhaps it revealed answers you had been seeking for decades.

Today, I'm able to bring my dreams into reality and share my story with you. Today, I am in a healthy and loving marriage. Today, I respect myself on a deeper level than ever before. In reflecting back on that period in my life, I didn't know how I was going to make it through. Yet, the person I am today is because of the work I did to walk through that pain and sorrow.

LESSON SIX—Learn to accept all aspects of yourself. The good, the bad, and the ugly.

As humans, we're great at accepting the parts of ourselves we label as good or lovable or "right." It's the shadow we don't want to look at. However, the truth is that when we integrate the two sides of ourselves, it creates the wholeness of who we are. It isn't easy work, but it is possible. I know because I did it.

Like most of you, I didn't want to look at my shadow. But I also intuitively knew that in my shadow I would find the wisdom I needed to heal and move forward with my life. I wanted to be a whole person. I wanted to show up in the world as "all of me." So, I dug in and started being rigorously honest about my behaviors and where I was hiding any part of myself.

- I looked for situations and circumstances where I was not taking responsibility for myself. And then, instead of hiding from what I saw, I *started changing my behavior and taking the needed responsibility.*
- I learned about codependency and sought help in making needed changes.

- I figured out what I liked, wanted and needed, instead of defaulting to the likes, needs and wants of others.
- I asked myself, "What are my dreams?" And then I began to pursue those dreams.
- I practiced forgiving myself and healing the shame and guilt that was keeping my stuck.

The more I was willing to look at all sides of me, and the more I worked on deeply loving and forgiving myself, the more I became a fully integrated human being. And today, I feel whole. Today, I like who I see in the mirror.

I recently had lunch with Rob—the man I almost drove into a semi-truck over—and he offered me the most beautiful mirror of all.

"Brenda, the reason we are sitting here today is because of all the forgiveness work you've done. If it wasn't for you, we wouldn't have this friendship today and I'm so grateful."

With tears in his eyes, he continued.

"But I still feel bad for all the hurt I caused you."

I reached across the table and took his hands in mine and looked him in the eyes.

"Hey … I've already forgiven you. When are you going to forgive yourself?

And I meant it.

Because, in that moment, I realized I was living the life I desire. I was no longer dependent on him. The "graspy" energy was no longer present. I had moved on, learning from the experience, dove deep into the pain, and came out the other side with love still in my heart.

I had finally, fully forgiven myself.

I knew this was true because I could never have invited him to forgive himself if I had not already forgiven him, and more importantly, if I had not forgiven myself.

Over ten years ago, I began training as a Radical Forgiveness Master Coach. That training helped me forgive myself, and then, miraculously, it helped me forgive Rob. Today, we are friends. Our friendship is mutually respectful, loving and kind. He cheers for my personal growth, professional achievement, and often attend my talks. And, he fully supports the telling of this story.

Dear once, forgiveness is powerful. It can loosen magnetic holds and reveal honest mirrors. It can free you from the shame, guilt and pain you carry so that you can create the life you desire. When you can do that, it ripples out all around you.

I wish you radical forgiveness.

Because when we forgive ourselves, we create a forgiving world.

⋯ ABOUT BRENDA REISS

Brenda Reiss, a celebrated Forgiveness Coach, keynote speaker, and author, has become a beacon of hope for those entangled in the grips of shame, resentment, and self-sabotage. With a profound journey marked by overcoming self-imposed limitations and victimhood, Brenda has transformed her life through the powerful practice of self-forgiveness. Her personal experiences with neglect and the quest for approval taught her the importance of breaking free from past traumas and toxic relationships, lessons she now passionately passes on to her clients. Today, Brenda is known not just for her books and talks but for her role as a Relationship Transformation coach. She empowers her clients by guiding them from a state of doubt and unworthiness to one of clarity, abundance, and freedom, enabling them to share their passions with the world. Her approach is deeply compassionate, focusing on liberating individuals so they can lead lives unbounded by their pasts. When she is not speaking or coaching, Brenda finds joy in hiking, reading extensively to broaden her knowledge, and spending quality time with her grandchildren and pets. These activities not only bring her personal joy but also enrich her coaching by providing continuous personal growth and grounding. Brenda's life is a testament to the power of rewriting one's narrative. Through her work as the Forgiveness Coach, she ignites the potential within her clients, inspiring them to redefine their lives and embrace the strength within. Her story and coaching encourage others to explore beyond their perceived limits and to discover the possibilities of a life led with heart and courage. Whether on stage, through her podcasts, or in one-on-one sessions, Brenda Reiss remains a guiding light to all who seek transformation.

Website: *http://brendareisscoaching.com*
Facebook: *https://www.facebook.com/Brenda.Reiss.Coach*
Instagram: *https://www.instagram.com/brendareisscoaching*
LinkedIn: *https://www.linkedin.com/in/brenda-reiss-3089031*
YouTube: *www.youtube.com/@BrendaReissCoaching*

5 ···· HIGH SELF-WORTH FOR BUILDING HIGH NET WORTH

by Tresa Leftenant

Ladies, we have a problem. Of the twenty-two million Americans (Zippia 2023) who are categorized as millionaires, only one third of them are women. This chapter will give you powerful tools and insights on how you can improve your prospects of becoming one of them.

There are many well-known reasons for the wealth gap between men and women, let's review them here:

- the earnings gap is stubbornly slow to narrow
- women often lack confidence with investing
- career interruptions for childbearing and caring for older parents
- lower retirement savings due to lower income
- our money needs to last longer because we live longer
- fewer women own property
- less access to loans and other financial resources
- entrenched discrimination practices in institutions

Addressing this wealth gap requires a comprehensive approach that considers both financial literacy and individual empowerment. In this chapter we will explore my perspective on the ingredients required for unprecedented levels of financial success.

Why would you listen to me?

I've been a Certified Financial Planner (CFP®) since 1990 and opened my own financial planning and wealth management company in 2003. I am a Certified Trainer of Jack Canfield's Success Principles and a Behavioral Finance Advisor (BFA™). But more importantly, I have reinvented my own financial life from tens of thousands in negative net-worth to a seven-figure net-worth and counting.

In this chapter, I'll tell my story and reveal seven steps for you to consider applying to your financial journey. My hope is that something I will share in the next few pages will grab your attention in a new way and motivate you to a whole new perspective on your money and life.

The following seven steps are only part of the pathway I followed during my reinvention; a course I now call "The Wealthy Woman Blueprint."

Step 1—Realize You are the Change You are Waiting For
Step 2—Accept That Change Is Inevitable so You Might as Well

Choose It

Step 3—Connect to and Enlighten Your Inner Power Qualities

Step 4—Stop Hiding Behind the Lies They Tell You About You

Step 5—Know Your Value and Stand in Your Power

Step 6—Stop Thinking You Can't and Develop a Positive Money Mindset

Step 7—Charge Ahead with a Simple and Effective Financial Planning Skillset

STEP ONE—Realize You are the Change You are Waiting For

Creating wealth has always been a goal of mine, but it wasn't until I had a huge epiphany in my forties that I found the right path. It started on a Tuesday afternoon as I was driving home in the middle of a workday during a wild Colorado thunderstorm. The crashing thunder and resulting downpour mirrored the storm of emotions pulsing through my body. The tears flowing down my face matched the raindrops pelting the windshield outside.

I pulled over to the side of the road and let myself howl.

It felt like years of stuffed pain erupting like a volcano out of my soul. That morning, on the way to work, I had dreams of receiving a coveted executive leadership position with a much needed and sizeable pay raise. All my problems would be solved by the announcement and my heart was brimming with excitement. But by afternoon, my hopes and dreams were dashed as my boss did his best to gently let me down.

Perhaps you, too, remember a day when everything in your life changed. An experience so unexpected that you would never see your life in the same way again. Losing out on that big promotion felt like hitting a brick wall going ninety miles an hour. I had believed so completely that it was the new start that I so desperately needed. As I sobbed and looked out of that rain-soaked window, my eyes drifted up to the sky.

"Why do I keep experiencing the same problems over and over again?" I asked out loud.

The Epiphany That Changed My Life

Suddenly a new thought jumped into my mind, as if from a bolt of lightning from above. It was so shockingly clear that I sucked in my breath and my tears instantly stopped. I could clearly see that in all the vast number of messes in my life, I was the common denominator. I was an expert at blaming everyone else for my problems, but in that moment, I felt the truth that it was my choices, my actions that had led to years of deep unhappiness and financial struggle.

STEP TWO—Accept That Change Is Inevitable so You Might as Well Choose It

At age forty, I had already been divorced three times. My financial situation included a good salary, but my net-worth was negative as I had tens of thousands of dollars of credit card debt. I was a single parent of two young children who needed attention that I struggled to provide. I coped with my feelings of hopelessness, shame, and guilt by drinking too much, shopping too often, and blaming everyone else for my troubles. But in that moment, I couldn't deny the truth of this new revelation.

As my tears dried up, I spoke again.

"If I'm the reason that my life isn't working, what do I do now? I don't know how to change things. Please, just give me some guidance and I promise to do whatever comes my way."

But I felt powerless to do anything differently. It felt like I was drowning under a dump truck of troubles. After all, I was a financial advisor and my shame about my financial woes ran deep, not to mention the pain from the last fifteen years of dashed dreams from three failed marriages. I had been in the money business since I got my first summer job at my hometown bank. My father was an executive at the bank, and my dream was to climb the corporate ladder and make him proud.

And there I was, in the middle of my life, facing the truth about the poor choices that had led me to hitting the glass ceiling. As I drove away from the office and my boss's bad news, I saw no options ahead that would dig me out of my financial hole and relationship woes.

Choosing to Change

After I made it clear to the Universe that I was open to change; within a week I was guided to a personal growth workshop titled "Self-Esteem for Teens." Although I wasn't totally clear what self-esteem actually was, I felt an inner recognition that this could be helpful for my children, and for me. We enrolled in the weekend course and the rest, they say, is history. My twenty-five-year self-development journey had magically begun.

Not too long after I promised that I would follow any sign, I attended a Success Path seminar and was introduced to Jack Canfield's (author of *The Chicken Soup for The Soul* series) audiobook titled, *How to Build High Self Esteem.* The instructor encouraged us to buy the cassette series, and again, I felt an inner nudge that there was something I needed to learn from Mr. Canfield. As I drove away from the seminar that day, I pushed the first cassette into my player. Right away, Jack began telling the powerful story of the Golden Buddha. You may know the story, so here is a shortened version of the tale.

In 1957, an entire monastery in Thailand was being relocated. As the monks were moving a nine-foot-tall clay Buddha, a large crack was discovered. The statue was originally built in 1403 and covered in clay to protect it from an invading army. For over five hundred years, the clay Buddha was thought to be unimportant and without value, until the day a monk noticed an inner light. And as the old clay began to fall away, its true brilliance and value shone through. A monk noticed a golden light emanating from the crack. He began to chip away the clay until a statue of solid gold was revealed, later valued at over $250 million, an even more substantial fortune in those days than it is today.

Jack says we all have a Golden Buddha inside of us, our inner core of greatness and potential that may be hidden beneath layers of self-doubt, fear and limiting beliefs that stop us from pursuing a life of abundance, meaning and joy. This story is a metaphor about the process of uncovering our inner being's true power for growth, love and prosperity. When we chip away our own layers of clay, we recognize and embrace our inner greatness, and the power to do, be or have whatever we imagine, even if we think it's impossible.

STEP THREE—Connect to and Enlighten Your Inner Power Qualities

If you resonate with this story, perhaps you sense the presence of your own inner Golden Buddha. I refer to my Golden Buddha as my Inner Being— the spark of life that animates my body and is connected to all things and all people. My inner being carries powerful and valuable assets that were installed at my birth, including curiosity, imagination, playfulness and creativity.

You and I have natural stores of wonder, inventiveness, wisdom, humor, vitality, sensitivity and flexibility. And even more exciting are the abundant feelings of joy and love that can be tapped with the ease of our next thought.

It took some time before I embraced how priceless I truly am, how my valuable inner assets are meant to be used on my journey to create a happy and wealthy life. Once I really got it, I was filled with a passion to help other women embrace their inner powers for changed their mindset and upgraded their skillset with money.

The Key is Self-Worth

Why is self-esteem (self-worth) such a core foundational ingredient for building financial wealth? Let's begin with a clear definition:

Self-worth, or self-esteem, is a psychological concept that pertains to an individual's overall sense of their own value and worth as a person. It is the belief that you are worthy, valuable, and deserving of respect, love, and acceptance, by yourself and others.

In those early years of self-development, I realized that many of my choices in life were primarily due to low self-esteem. My parent's generation weren't aware of the importance of teaching children about their value. It took a few years of re-parenting myself to believe that no matter how many mistakes I make, or what other people think about me, I am valuable just because I exist.

Even as parents now raise their children with more empowering messages, many women still hold on to a core belief that they aren't as worthy or capable as men. These debilitating beliefs are perpetuated and enforced by societal and familial messages passed down through the generations. Without an unshakable belief in our own inherent value, we won't believe that we deserve the life we dream about. In my forty-year career as a financial advisor to women with many different levels of net-worth, I've observed a direct correlation between self-worth and net-worth. Yet many women don't understand, or aren't willing to consider, how improving their self-worth might be the key to breaking free of financial woes.

STEP FOUR—Stop Hiding Behind the Lies They Tell You About You

Let's consider how historic messages have taken a toll on a woman's self-worth. For instance, The Equal Pay Act, which was aimed at abolishing wage disparity based on sex, wasn't passed until 1963! But still it has been sixty years that women have been given the opportunity to be seen as equal at work. According to a 2019 article from CNBC, the wage gap between men and women averages twenty percent, meaning women get paid eighty cents for every dollar men earn. In the last ten years, the pay gap only narrowed about two percent, and if performance stays consistent with past decades, it will take one hundred years to reach equal pay, according to Goldman Sachs.

Let's look deeper into these statistics. According to a 2023 Forbes article, the average pay gap between men and women is seventeen percent, however in the legal industry a man earns on average of fifty-nine percent more than a woman. Women of color are among the lowest paid workers in rural areas, making just 56 percent for every dollar a rural white man makes. To shed some light on the numbers, a twenty-year-old woman just starting full-time year-round work stands to lose $407,760 over a forty-year career compared to her male counterpart. This reality takes away the choices a woman can make to ensure her financial future and create the same levels of wealth that men enjoy.

Yes, feelings of low self-worth have roots in historical patriarchy; where men believe they should have more power and control than women. The mistaken belief that men are superior to women has persisted for generations in the minds of both men and women. And it isn't just at work that we have been taught to think less of ourselves. Men and women have allowed this unequal power dynamic to continue to exist in our marriages, churches, friendship circles and family structures.

The Truth will Set You Free

I invite you to explore if there are any places in your life where you continue to believe the lies that have kept women small and subservient for hundreds of years, especially in your relationship and actions with money.

The mountains of credit card debt that I created in my twenties and thirties was built on the back of comparing myself to men who had more money than me. I coped with feelings of inadequacy by "showing-off" my fake wealth by buying expensive clothes, new cars, and home furnishings which I denied that I couldn't afford. I desperately needed approval from those I perceived as "better, smarter, braver" than me because I couldn't generate any approval for myself. I believed the way I looked, where I lived, and who I hung out with determined my value. It took an experience that brought me to my knees to see that my true value could only be found within myself.

STEP FIVE—Know Your Value and Stand in Your Power

To make the same, or more, as your male counterparts, to build your million dollar and higher net-worth, you must believe that you are absolutely equal to the men and women around you. Don't misunderstand me, I know that women *are* making progress, but where do you stand on these questions? Are you accepting less than you deserve because you secretly don't believe you bring as much to the table as a man? Are you settling for just feeling financially secure instead of taking steps to build a multi-million-dollar net-worth on your own? Are you sitting in the back seat of your family's financial car, letting your husband/partner do all the driving?

Your Power is Unstoppable

If you know deep down that your self-worth could use a boost, take heart. To feel a high sense of self-worth every day, you just need to take a stand for your value by developing the powerful inner gifts you already have inside. Once you feel your inner power, you'll be unstoppable.

Commit 100% to Your Path

I can confidently say that what happened to me that Tuesday in the rain when I didn't get that promotion was a gift from God. My willingness to open my mind and ask clearly for guidance engaged the Law of Attraction, like a key that turned a golden lock. I was almost immediately guided to a whole new perspective on life, and my place in it.

I discovered that my Inner Being is as priceless as The Golden Buddha, and it is the source of my power. When I chose to be 100 percent committed to my evolving path, I received a priceless invitation. I now can answer the question, "who do I want to be and what do I want to experience during the rest of my life?" I walked through the doorway of reinvention and everything in my life began to change almost immediately.

STEP SIX—Stop Thinking You Can't and Develop a Positive Money Mindset

With each new breakthrough, mindset shift and self-awareness habit, I slowly changed myself and my experiences. It wasn't easy to change my thinking, I had the same negative thoughts that you may have:

1. Who do you think you are?
2. Don't get too big for your britches!
3. Other people can, but I can't.

I began to gain more awareness about how old patterns of thought contributed to the painful experiences in my past. As I connected the dots between thoughts and results, I consciously created a whole new mindset, one that supported taking the right steps to reach my goals.

I began to truly believe in my own worth, and noticed I could also grow other Golden Buddha qualities—such as self-confidence, courage and self-respect. I began to see how all my inner assets, available at my command, prepared me mentally and emotionally for the bigger risks I now could choose to take as I pursued my dreams. With more positive thinking and higher levels of inner confidence and courage, I invested an inheritance in my dream of owning a vacation home in Sun Valley, Idaho. I spent ten years enjoying the annual Sun Valley Wellness Festival—a wellness gathering focused on educating attendees on physical, mental and spiritual well-being. Owning a property there contributed to being hired as a speaker on financial wellness, which led to other speaking opportunities and meeting more prospective clients.

It was my inner assets of curiosity, inventiveness and wisdom that motivated me to open my own wealth management practice in 2003. During my corporate career I wondered if there was a more ethical financial planning experience that I could create for women, one where I was accountable to my clients, not a big corporation. By the time I took the leap from a six-figure salary with benefits to my big vision with no income, my stores of self-esteem were secure. Being an entrepreneur is unpredictable, transformative and deeply fulfilling. It challenged me to let go of my need to be perfect and trust that being my authentic self is exactly what my client's need to reach their own wealthy life goals.

Besides paying off all that shameful credit card debt and creating a multimillion dollar net worth, I enjoy a romance novel relationship with my fourth husband of twenty-four years (and counting!), and our three children are happily pursuing their dreams. I'm not an overnight success story, but over time I learned to love myself and navigate life with a set of tools that truly support the creation of a profoundly happy and abundant life.

In my financial planning practice, I talk to women every day who have low self-worth and negative beliefs about their abilities with money. In my book *Reinventing HER—Helping Women Plan, Pursue and Capitalize on Their Next Chapter,* I outline many of the tools that I used to transform my financial life. I began integrating life coaching into my financial advice to help women connect the dots between self-worth and net worth. It's a marriage between the right and left brain, understanding how to navigate personal finance concepts along with enhancing the inner resources that can give women the edge they deserve on their wealth quest.

STEP SEVEN—Charge Ahead with a Simple and Effective Financial Planning Skillset

It's important to keep the whole idea of money in perspective—it's only a tool we use like a hammer or a makeup brush. Money doesn't have to be an end in itself, but rather a means to achieve various goals and objectives. It facilitates transactions fostering economic activity and wealth creation. It also provides freedom and choice, offering new opportunities. Money can also be a tool for positive social change and provide a cushion in case of emergencies. It can provide more flexibility with time management, as well as support innovation, research and bring new ideas to fruition. Money can lift people out of poverty through education and skill development and raise every person's quality of life through comfortable living conditions, leisure activities, travel, and the enjoyment of extraordinary experiences. The role of money in our lives is the achievement of broader life goals and not as the ultimate end.

Practicing a financial planning skillset is much easier when your inner power qualities are charged up and ready to go. When your self-worth is high, you automatically make different decisions, about your money and in other areas of your life as well.

I provide my female clients with an easy to implement six-step financial planning skillset:

1. **Earn it**—set goals and an action plan to earn what you deserve now and continue to increase your earnings throughout your career.
2. **Save it**—set goals and action plans to create your vision for an ideal life, such as buying property, educating children, starting a business, traveling the world, and building a nest egg to pay for your chosen lifestyle when you choose to cut back or stop working.
3. **Spend it**—design a monthly plan for spending your money on the areas of life that support your personal short and long-term goals.
4. **Grow it**—navigate the changing economy and markets with investment strategies that suit your comfort level with risk and grow your money for the timing of individual long-term goals.
5. **Protect it**—guard your hard-earned money from big risks such as premature death, health events, long term care, and paying too much tax.
6. **Share it**—design a plan for gifting to charities, family, and important causes, and set up legal documents for passing your money on to others.

If you are still with me, I hope you found my philosophy helpful. You *can* become one of the next generation of women millionaires by knowing your value, rejecting the lies, creating a positive money mindset and implementing a simple financial planning skillset. See money as a tool and use it with confidence, clarity, and commitment to your goal. You can be the change you are looking for and boldly make your dreams come true. Let's reinvent ourselves into the women we want to become, pursuing the life we were born to live.

··· ABOUT TRESA LEFTENANT

Tresa Leftenant is a Certified Financial Planner (CFP®) and Behavioral Finance Advisor (BFA™) with over four decades of comprehensive financial planning and wealth advisory experience. She's also a Certified Canfield Trainer of The Success Principles, a popular speaker, podcaster and transformation facilitator. Tresa left a successful career in corporate America to open a private financial advisory practice and is fiercely committed to guiding women to pursue their version of a wealthy and purposeful life. She empowers women to build and manage the financial resources they need to support their dreams, through education programs that highlight the intersection between a positive money mindset and a committed financial planning skillset. Tresa's masterwork *Reinventing Her – Helping Women Plan, Pursue, and Capitalize on Their Next Chapter* (available on Amazon), is a handbook for women who are ready to change their financial life. She openly shares her own transformation with money, relationships and career, and encourages women to upgrade their life by learning and living the steps she created to change hers. In her forties, Tresa was a chronic shopaholic with tens of thousands of dollars in credit card debt and three failed marriages. One day she experienced a life-changing epiphany and dedicated herself to personal development to turn a negative net-worth into seven figures and counting, and enjoys a romance-novel relationship with her current husband of twenty-four years. She knows from personal experience how to turn around unwanted life results and has the training to facilitate the best life changing strategies available today with her clients. Learn more about her programs and women's wealth discussion circles at *www.awealthylife.com*.

Website: *https://www.awealthylifeforher.com*
Website: *https://www.reinventingher.com*
Business Facebook Page: *www.facebook.com/ReinventingHer*
LinkedIn: *https://www.linkedin.com/in/tresadleftenant*

6 ⋯ REMARKABLE

by Remalynn Muñoz

*When it is all finished you will see that it was never random. In
the meantime, have faith all is happening for a reason.
Look for the lessons, the gifts, the bridge you are to take
to get to yourself where you need to be.* -Karen Salmansohn

A few years ago, I participated in a seven-day personal development
retreat. One of the activities on the agenda was the trust fall. When I heard
"trust fall," I thought of a person—*me*—falling backward and being on the
same level ground as the catcher. It caused hesitation in me to be one
hundred percent fully into the activity. The large group moved to the
activity area, and I saw six-foot tall platforms and didn't think much of it.

As the facilitators gave the instructions, it became very clear this was not the typical trust fall, where all participants are on the ground

We were separated into a few small groups and told that the catchers needed to be in a very tight position, strong landing base foundation for the one falling. We had to trust and look out for each other so that our members wouldn't get hurt; the ones falling *and* the ones catching.

It was my turn and as I walked up the stairs slowly, with shaky legs and my heart pounding, I felt scared. I imagined myself falling backwards from a six-foot tall platform into the arms of people I'd met only a couple of days before. At the top of the platform, I was met by the facilitator, where he gave me more instructions and prepared me for safety reasons. He then led me to the edge of the platform, turned me around, and looked me in the eye.

"Who are you afraid to trust? Others or yourself?" he asked.

I thought about it.

"Both," I whispered.

I took a deep breath, closed my eyes, and after what felt like minutes of me standing there, I let myself fall. Mid-fall, fear overwhelmed me, and I let out a scream. Thoughts ran through my head. "

Please, please, please catch me. I don't want to fail and get hurt! I landed safely in my team's arms, tears flowed freely. They stayed silent and still, as they held me while I lay in their arms. They gave me a moment to feel; to soak in and process what had just happened.

As I recall that event, tears still well up in my eyes today. It's surprising how significant that moment was for me. At the time, my life was clouded with doubt, skepticism and fear. Yet, in the midst of that activity, I realized the importance of setting aside those feelings to *truly* experience trust. Seeds of trust are planted within us at unexpected times in our lives. They sprout and grow at the perfect timing for significance and beauty. To me, that day planted the seed of trust for others and myself. It grows within me and gets stronger as I heal each wounded layer. As Amy Atherson once said, "Be brave. Let go. Trust the process. Allow the universe to reveal its beautiful plan."

I also didn't expect to walk away from a high school basketball game with a message, but life has a funny way of surprising us. One day I was sitting in the stands, waiting for the game to begin when something caught my eye. The team's uniform. On the back of the jersey, instead of the usual school or player last name, the uniform had three letters: TTP. I couldn't help but wonder what that meant. Phrases ran through my mind, mostly me trying to connect words that could possibly stand for "TTP." None of it made sense. My curiosity wouldn't subside.

"What does 'TTP' stand for?" I asked the woman beside me.

"Trust the process," she replied.

At that moment, it was a message I needed to hear. And it was clear.

"Remalynn, trust the process. Trust *me*."

God has a great sense of humor. His timing is impeccable. We just have to be open to receiving it.

Trust the process? Me? How am I supposed to trust when I don't know what will happen? What is the process supposed to look like, for me to trust it? When is said "process" supposed to end? What if I mess it all up? Should I do this? Should I do that? What am I supposed to do to make it happen?

Whoa!

Somebody, quiet my mind!

Questions swirling in my mind, feeding my overthinking, fear and anxiousness. They were holding me back from allowing things to unfold as they're meant to, in their own time and in their way. Trust the process. Even when the path ahead seems to be unclear or impossible. It doesn't mean to sit still or stay stagnant. Be brave enough to learn the lesson. Let go to grow the mind. Allow yourself to be.

The voice is the amplifier of the mind, heart, and soul.

Let me repeat that.

The voice is the amplifier of the mind, heart, and soul.

Pain isn't always visible, and it can run deeper than one can ever imagine. For me, the healing process was many thoughts of, *I have to deal with this pain, again? How many layers does this pain have?*

The unspoken words of a child are heard in the screams of an adult. As a child, I learned that I wouldn't be allowed to express myself fully. When I spoke, I felt like I wasn't being heard. As I grew, each time I was silenced it became a layer of hurt that turned into screams of anger. Looking back, I allowed everyone else's story to diminish mine. When I finally reached my limit of hurt, I raised my voice and screamed ... and I didn't listen. My voice got louder because my pain got stronger. When I tried to give my side of the story, I felt it was dismissed. The message I received, true or not, was as such: anxiety was reserved for others, panic attacks were uncalled for, and breakdowns were attention-seeking. It hurt to see others being consoled, understood and cared for during their times of need.

Don't I deserve to be heard and seen as well?

I turned to isolation. Mentally, physically and emotionally.

Healing. That was a journey of its own, not a walk in the park by any means. I found myself stuck in the endless loop of replaying scenarios in my head, always telling myself what I should have done differently. Each misstep became a weight, dragging me deeper into self-doubt and self-blame. Instead of offering myself kindness and understanding, I was relentless in my criticism. I also felt alone in my process of healing. Instead of giving myself a break, I'd beat myself up—constantly worrying that if I made someone mad, they'd cut me off and leave me. After any argument, my mind would spiral in self-doubt.

Why'd you say that? Now they won't like you anymore. They might even leave you. You won't have anyone. Better keep your mouth shut next time.

I used to think that resolving my issues was as simple as identifying and fixing what was wrong within me, and to never allow it to surface again. I found myself feeling defeated when history kept repeating itself. It gave fuel to the "there is something wrong with me" message I often sent myself. For the longest time, I allowed life to simply unfold without actively steering it. It was more like being on cruise control, except without the control part. I didn't feel like myself. I felt disconnected from my own life. I feared losing what was important to me. I forgot I was important. I was scared to be me. I was lost in the darkness of self-identity.

I punished myself daily with thoughts of how much I failed in life.

All of this stemmed from this deep-rooted fear of not being lovable or worthy. It was a little voice in my head sabotaging me and always reminding me of my flaws. That voice of self-criticism just kept coming back, louder each time, like some broken record stuck on repeat. It was Marianne Williamson who once said, "The spiritual journey is the unlearning of fear and the acceptance of love."

There are two moments in my life that will forever be etched in my mind and heart. They both play a pivotal part in my healing journey. The first was at the same personal development retreat, but during a different activity. And it was a perfect recipe of fear, bravery, trust, release, compassion and beauty.

Picture standing at the edge of a towering cliff, with nothing but vast acres of open land stretching out before you in a 180-degree panoramic view. Before going to the edge, the facilitator took a moment to talk to me. I am afraid of heights so just thinking about being on the edge of a cliff scares the crap out of me. She could see the fear in me and what she said to me after giving the instructions was liberating. She had told me that I could yell whatever I wanted to say to the wind. And not to be hesitant.

I could say or yell whatever I wanted without interruptions or judgment.

Before I was to go on the path, I was put in a harness for safety. My turn came up and I walked to the end of the path to meet the safety personnel to connect to a safety line. I was walking on the path, my legs shaking just like the other activity. Okay, my whole body was shaking. My hands were clammy. *Could I really do this? Am I really doing this?* When I met the safety personnel: his energy was calming, and I became calm. He asked if I was ready, and I felt the excitement again.

Yes, I was ready!

I felt that I could trust him to keep me safe. I walked to the edge of the cliff, positioned myself as instructed, stood strong on my feet, opened my arms to my sides like they were wings, and when told to do so, I slowly leaned forward.

"I have you," someone behind me said.

I don't know how much I leaned forward, it felt like it was at least forty-five degrees, but it wasn't. I was surprised to discover it was less when I saw a photo later, but the degree I leaned does not matter. At that moment, I trusted, overcame a fear, and welcomed the chance to speak my truth. It felt so weird to yell out to the open space at first.

"Is that all you have inside you?" one of the facilitators asked.

So, I yelled as loud as I could. I swore at the ones that hurt me the most. I knew that was my chance for the little girl in me to feel like she was someone and in control.

I gave my pain a voice.

The second moment still gives me goosebumps when I think about it. I was overwhelmed with emotions that day. I was having a breakdown and crying out of desperation from the depth of my core, unsure of what to do next. I questioned if life was even worth continuing. I felt so small and insignificant. I wanted a comforting hug, a reassuring voice to tell me it was okay to feel lost and that I wasn't alone. I didn't get that hug, I didn't hear a reassuring voice telling me it was okay to feel, and I *was* alone. But as I lay there, overcome with feelings of unworthiness and doubt, a voice broke through the chaos.

"Remalynn, my child. I am here for you."

It felt so surreal. God's presence enveloped me, calming my turmoil. With eyes closed, I saw him approaching, arms open wide, radiating love and acceptance. His words echoed in my mind, offering comfort, support, and reassurance. In his embrace, I found a sense of security and peace. My breathing slowed, clarity replaced confusion and my body relaxed. It was a moment of profound connection, a reminder that I was never truly alone. Rachel Hollis says, "By embracing your calling and refusing to hide your glow, you wouldn't just make your world brighter, you'd light the way for the women who come behind you."

As I reflected on my own self-development journey, I was having a hard time coming up with the words to relay my truth in it and describe it. It's not about the classes I've taken, how long I took them for, or listing certificates I've earned. It is a continuous journey that I will be on for as long as I am on this earth.

If I was to paint a picture of my healing journey it would be of a cave. One side is in a dark shaded area, overran with lackluster vegetation, muddy ground, animals are in hiding, and the energy is heavy and unwelcoming. On the other side, the sun shining brightly, a beautiful waterfall pouring into a clear body of water, healthy vegetation, animals joyful in their environment, and the energy is light and feeling of home. In this cave, I would be in the middle, wondering what my next step would be. I can go back to what was familiar, the shady side, but nothing would change, and I would not be my genuine self. Or I can go towards a direction I know nothing about and scared to do so. But I hear it's liberating.

What do I *want* to do? I sit there feeling very lost. Contemplating and indecisive. I sit still for a long time. Life on either side of the cave is moving without me. What I know is that the familiar route no longer is comfortable for me. Something within me is asking for changes. My heart is ready, but my mind is scared.

Taking that initial step toward healing was daunting, however, I needed to start somewhere. When I was ready, I had a very hard time looking for a therapist. I had three wants: for the therapist to be a woman, her focused field to be childhood trauma, and Asian. I didn't think I was asking for too much. After a couple of months searching for one, unsuccessfully, I settled for what was available to me and started from there. I think this was when the spark of my calling happened. I felt discouraged, I almost quit before I started. I found a therapist who was a woman, who's focus was on childhood trauma, but wasn't Asian. It wasn't a deal breaker, but there is something to be said about not having to explain certain things like cultural norms, behavior and thoughts. I knew I wanted to support women as they go through life's challenges, and I wanted women who look like me to have choices. I just didn't know what that would look like.

The idea of becoming a Life Coach never crossed my mind initially. Owning my own business seemed like a distant dream. Inspired by my transformative experiences, I felt called to empower women facing similar struggles. I wanted to support someone going through the emotions of transformation. Especially when it feels like nothing has changed and they want to quit. I can empathize with them. I've wanted to quit many times and I am glad I didn't. In the moment, it was hard to see the work is worth it. But ... I am worth it. They are worth it.

I will be honest and say there will be difficult times in your journey, however, you have survived difficult times. It's time to thrive through challenging times. But you matter. Your voice matters. You are not alone. Perhaps, like me, you too have felt unheard and unseen, navigating life on autopilot. Most of us desire to feel self-love, self-validation, self-identity, and self-peace; instead of living as silenced voices longing to be heard.

This is at the heart of Remarkable Transformation.

So, what kind of coach am I? An awesome one (insert laughter). Jokes aside. I am an Accountability Coach. I provide women with a safe place to explore and be who they are. I support and encourage them by providing a nurturing environment for their personal growth. I walk with them as they break free from limitations, unlock their full potential, and embrace the abundance they truly deserve. I walk with women as they maneuver life's challenges. I celebrate the small victories as much as the big ones. I am the cheerleader in the in-between space of new beginnings and their awakened true self. Their remarkable transformation is an inspiration to others.

Awaken

The slumber has come to an end.

No longer hide your God-given gift.

Allow your light to shine.

Open your heart to give.

Free your mind to receive.

Your words are to be voiced.

Awaken your hidden spirit.

Beautiful women …

… be *you*.

··· ABOUT REMALYNN MUÑOZ

As an Accountability Coach, I'm not only dedicated to helping others; I'm also the founder and CEO of Remarkable Transformation. Growing up as a first-generation Filipino American, I've had to navigate and blend my family's traditions and culture with the new experiences I encountered, facing both challenges and rewards along the way. As a mom of two grown children, I've had the privilege of raising them alongside our extended family. Now, the family has grown with the addition of a daughter-in-law, going through the journey called life. I'm a proud grandma to two grandsons who lovingly call me Ina, cherishing every moment with them as they bring light and laughter into everyone's lives. When I'm not working, you can find me dancing enjoying the freedom of movement and expression, or finding peace by the ocean's calming waves. Inspired by my own journey of change, I now help others facing similar struggles. I firmly believe that everyone deserves to embrace who they truly are. Through Remarkable Transformation, I provide a safe and nurturing environment for personal growth. I understand the struggles of transformation firsthand and am committed to helping you navigate them with confidence and resilience. With my support, you can overcome self-doubt, find clarity in your goals, and take meaningful steps towards a brighter future.

Instagram - *@remarkable.transformation*
Facebook - *Remarkable Transformation*
Website - *remalynn.com*
Email - *remarkabletransformation@gmail.com*

7 ··· A BIRD ON TOP OF A CAGE, SINGING

by Dani Green

Many years ago, I went to a fundraising event and from across the room I saw a decorative birdcage. I first noticed that the sage green color would match our living room hearth. Then something caught my heart: a bird was on top of the cage, singing. I rushed across the room, put my bid number in the final square, and carried the birdcage for the rest of the evening.

I deeply longed to be a bird on top of the cage, singing, and somehow, I knew I was holding a future promise.

Lost

Years later, I doubted God was with me. At the time I was a staff pastor, so my feelings were problematic. I watched for signs and acted upon what I felt was true, but I felt lost. I could not go to work that day. I spent the prior evening trying not to cry at a church event. A good friend noticed my tears and suggested the book *The War of Art: Break Through the Blocks and Win Your Inner Creative Battles,* by Steven Pressfield. The next morning, I listened to the book for three hours and twenty-two minutes as I sat at my kitchen table. I found the words that instantly changed my psyche. "…the part we create from, that part is far deeper and stronger. The part we create from cannot be touched by anything our parents did or society did. That part is unsullied, uncorrupted, soundproof, waterproof, and bulletproof."

Found

Suddenly, I said, "I'm okay." Undeniably, I felt *deeply* okay. I realized I had always been okay—although I did not know it. And I would *always* be okay for eternity. Something inside of me changed. Before this moment, I was determined but unsure. I had always pushed forward but part of me wanted to run and hide. My circumstances would not change for another fourteen months, but I navigated that time differently than before. I had an inner calm that was new and stabilizing. I was on a new path.

From that day, I have genuinely learned to lead from within, from my Soul. As you read how my story and that of my clients continue with teachable moments, I trust you will also see a new path for yourself.

Namaste

One New Year's Eve evening, I left my church job and asked God, "What more is out here in the world for healing and transformation?"

I would soon find out.

In a few short weeks, we were traveling to India for our daughter's wedding. When I asked our son-in-law-to-be how to greet our new family, he answered, "Namaste." He explained namaste means "the divine in me greets the divine in you."

"That is the nicest thing anyone has ever said to me!" I thought.

My worldview changed.

In an instant, I saw everyone as Divine. The entire human family—past, present, and future is equal, loved, worthy, and Divine.

Obey Your Soul

After we returned from India, I listened to an audiobook called *The Science of Being Great* by Wallace Waddles. The author encourages us to "obey your soul." I shouted, "I knew it!" Something deep within knew this was true. Until this moment, I had not realized it was my Soul I discovered fifteen months ago sitting at my kitchen table!

I spent my life obeying those outside of me—my parents, siblings, teachers, bosses, pastors, husband and God. It was no wonder I felt so lost. I relied on so many outside influences I could not hear my innermost self. So, I began to obey my Soul. I had read the signs correctly all those months before. I was brave. Following those signs led me to today. It would be a while more before I understood the infinite power of my Soul.

The Next Step

I became an entrepreneur. As an ordained minister, I continued to officiate weddings and funerals. And I became a certified hypnotherapist. I went to a group hypnosis session, and since I have not eaten a graham cracker or an Oreo cookie, so I know hypnosis works!

In studying to become an Emotion Code practitioner, I learned the cells of our body are 99.99999 percent space from *The Emotion Code: How to Release Your Trapped Emotions for Abundant Health, Love and Happiness* by Bradley Nelson. Some scientists are beginning to call that space "spirit." Wow!

After many years of striving to be close to God, I realized every cell of my body is infused with the spirit of God. I began to feel more Divine! Divine Love is in each of us and with all of us, and it always has been and will always be. We no longer need to strive to feel close to God.

In 2018, with the help of a business coach, I created my concept of Soul Power. Since then, I live 24/7/365 with an expansive, powerful, and beautiful sense of my inner and infinite Soul motivating and empowering *everything* I do. Oh, my goodness, I am so amazing! No one and no circumstance will ever be able to diminish my Soul Power!

The Teacher in Me

Now that you know some of my story, I want to explain what is coming next. I have gathered some concepts that have made a world of difference in my mindset, worldview, and daily high-vibe lifestyle. I trust the following concepts will speak to you.

Soul Words

The concept of Soul became very important to me. Notice how often the concept is represented in articles, books, movies, and social media. Have you ever imagined your Soul? Being aware of your Soul reveals your constant and perfect connection to Divine Source. I have created a list of words to represent our Soul. You will see ancient and contemporary truths listed here. Meditate on these words to activate what is profoundly true for you.

Aliveness. Authentic Self. Awareness. Being. Consciousness. Contentment. Courage. Co-Creator. Divinity. Energy. Enlightenment. Essence. Eternity. Freedom. Genius. God-in-me. Greatness. Grounded. Happiness. Harmony. Hero. Higher power. Highest self. Home. I am. Identity. Immovable. Incorruptible. Indestructible. Infinite. Inner abiding. Inner guidance. Inner healer. Inmost being. Joy. The life. Life force. Light. Love. One. Peace. The pearl. Perfect self-expression. Presence. Pure. Refuge. Rest. Safe. Self-sovereignty. Sinless. Source. Still small voice. Strength. Suffering. Superconscious. Transformation. True purpose. True self. Truth. Unique. The way. Wholeness.

Your Soul is a place to rest when the outside world is disappointing, overwhelming, and stressful. Imagine the light of your Soul. Allow this healing light to fill and radiate beyond your body.

We Are Light

I came across an enlightening online article about biophotons. Our cells have light energy, which can be increased by focusing on light. Light energy can improve our immune system and provide healing. Jesus said, "You are the light of the world," in the book of Matthew in the Bible. We are all filled with light. Focus on your light to improve your life. As a mediation, I focus on the light of my Soul and send light energy to those who need it most. When I think of those trapped by confusion and obscurity, I trust my prayers make a difference.

Imagine the light of your Soul radiating past your skin to the space around you. Next, imagine the light of the sun, moon, and stars shining toward you. Somewhere in this space, your light joins with the light of the universe. You are infinite!

We Are Love

During meditation, the word "love" became written across my body like an invisible tattoo. The "L" covered my head and left arm, the "O" was across my heart, the "V" landed on my lower torso, and the "E" covered my legs and feet. I became *love* that day. Close your eyes and imagine *love* written across your body. Where and how is it written?

As a meditation, I focus on and fill my body with love and send it to those who need it most today. When I think of people feeling alone and sad, I know sending love brings healing. As I walk through my day, with a big smile, I turn around in a circle, saying in my mind, "I love you, I love you, I love you" to everything around me. Try it! Imagine love filling your body like a water glass overflowing into the space around you. Imagine the energy of love radiating from your body.

A 49-year-old female client was facing an "empty nest" and wondered what her new purpose should be. In a hypnosis session, I repeatedly asked, "What is more important?" She answered each question sincerely and realized she was simply and profoundly "an expression of love." With this new understanding, she instantly felt happy and close to God and realized any choice for her future would be fulfilling.

We Are Power

I don't know about you, but it has taken me a lifetime to realize how powerful I am. When I focus on the power of my Divine Soul, I feel more grounded, alive and empowered to fulfill my life purpose. Imagine your eternal power, which is beyond measure.

As a meditation, I focus on and recognize my inner and eternal power for good and send power to those who need it most today. Especially those despairing of life, they need power to make it through their difficult situation, moment by moment.

We Are Wisdom

Imagine your life as a path. You have inner wisdom for the next best step. At any given moment, we are all as able as we are, even on our worst day. Each cell of our body is infused with divine wisdom. When I began to know Jesus at age eight, my faith sometimes worked for me, and sometimes it did not. What if I missed God's will? On what path of destruction would I find myself? Yikes! I understand wisdom so differently now.

With my choices, I trust that infinite love, my Soul, and my humanity will work together to make the best of everything! "**To thine own self be true**" (Hamlet, act 1, scene 3, Shakespeare) represents how I live now. I no longer experience the weight of God or others watching my every move.

We had an Airbnb in our home. One afternoon, I received a text from a guest who explained his girlfriend had broken up with him and left. He decided to leave, too. I thought, "God, what can I say to bring comfort and clarity?" And then this came to me, "You are always on the best path." Wow, for the first time, I instantly understood that whatever path we are on is the best path. Infinite love is with us, ready to make the best of our choices and experiences.

Now I understand God's will allows me to do what I choose, whether I turn to the left or right, stop, or go back. Everything can be for my highest good and the highest good of others. Truth will be revealed.

Life-Giving or Life-Draining Emotions?

I consider whether my choices are life-giving or life-draining. I live with natural consequences. That's it. I am free from self-judgment! Thank God, the concept of sin has not entered my psyche since 2018.

Emotions are energy radiating measurably twelve feet from our body. As you read the following list, consider which emotions you want in your body and life. Release life-draining emotions through breath work, body movement, hand sweeps or hypnosis. Strengthen life-giving emotions through meditation, journaling, and touch.

The Map of Consciousness, in the book *Power vs. Force* by David R. Hawkins, lists the energetic frequency of emotions. Shame (20) is the lowest energy emotion, and enlightenment (1000) is the highest.

Emotions measuring under two hundred are life-draining. These emotions—starting with the lowest—are shame, guilt, apathy, grief, fear, desire, anger and pride. Emotions measuring two hundred and above are life-giving. These emotions—starting with the lowest—are courage, neutrality, willingness, acceptance, reason, love, joy, peace and enlightenment.

It is good to know what is above. Being in a higher emotional state benefits you, your family, your community, your country and the world. When people are really suffering, it can be hard to rise above it.

Our Atman and Jiva Soul

I found the following truths about our Soul in the book *How to Know God* by Deepak Chopra. We each have an eternal soul called *Atman* and an evolving soul that suffers with us called *Jiva.* The Jiva part of our Soul understands our humanity, including our actions. Our Atman soul can be called "The Eternal You!"

At first, I wondered if our Jiva Soul matures and grows more loving with each lifetime. Now I understand infinite love wants nothing less than to see us grow more loving toward each other every day. We are evolving toward love. Infinite love uses every good thing about us. We can also trust goodness is coming to us. Even if we make life-draining choices, eventually, we realize what we would rather want. We can walk away from the things that do not feel right. People who act violently do not know about their divinity, which is obscured by the pain of their ancestors, lives, circumstances, social environment, experiences, and even their religion. When we enter the realm after this one, we understand

and feel what our life has caused and are invited to heal. Some need more healing than others because we are all at different stages of evolution. Those who have been deeply hurt by a person are the most challenging circumstances to endure. We can trust they will see the truth of what they have done. Love will heal us all. Everything serves us.

The Kaleidoscope Principle

Often, when I speak with young people or adults facing a decision, they are stressed they might make the wrong choice. This led me to think about how we view decision-making. If you think of life as a blueprint, you might feel subject to fate. If you see life as a puzzle, you always search for the next missing piece. If you see life as a tapestry, you can feel entangled by details and have no idea what the tapestry looks like on the other side. Think of the beauty of a kaleidoscope. You can view life as a kaleidoscope. Whether you turn the dial forward or backward, you will see beautiful colors all falling together in an orderly way. Whether you take two steps forward or two steps back, you are still on your Perfect Path. You must turn the dial. Do not let fear stop you from taking action. To quote Eckhart Tolle, "If uncertainty is unacceptable to you, it turns into fear. If it is perfectly acceptable, it turns into increased aliveness, alertness, and creativity."

Life can seem uncertain, but we can trust the order Love provides. I feel so empowered to know I do not need to stress about my choices every day. I know my heart, intentions, and actions will make the difference they are supposed to make. I believe in love, timing, and karma.

Life As a Teacher

Our survival brain reminds us of past unhelpful actions, so we don't repeat them. These thoughts usually spiral into regret. However, we can turn regret around into a learning experience. If we could do things over again, we would do them differently. We can change the past by creating a different story in meditation or hypnosis.

As we look at the events where we feel we failed, we can ask ourselves, "What did I learn? And how did it make me stronger." You cannot fail. We learn so much from life! The events of your life have made you the person you are today. Find the gift that life teaches us! I have learned to be very observant of my own experiences and the experiences of others. I have made high-vibe, life-giving changes to my health since both of my parents died at sixty-seven years old from lifestyle health-related diseases.

Everything Belongs

Quoting an American Franciscan priest, Richard Rohr, "Everything belongs." We do not need to wonder why certain things did or did not happen; we can relax into the concept that everything belongs and find redeeming meaning and purpose in our circumstances.

My dad had to leave our family before I was one year old. My heart healed when I understood he always did his best. I moved to Washington state at age twelve with my twin sister to live with my dad and his family; they saved my life. My mom was bipolar and self-medicated with alcohol. She was able to maintain a job to provide for her four children. We became best friends after I became a mom.

Everything belongs.

We Are Always Doing Our Best

We have heard the adage, "If you know better, do better." However, I am haunted by circumstances where I knew better but could not do better. The bottom line is that everyone is doing the best they are able to do. When we can accept our ability level every moment—past and present—we are relieved of guilt and shame.

Infinite love accepts us, always. When we accept ourselves and others as they are, we have more peace and radiate peace to the human family, the planet, and beyond.

As a client-centered hypnotherapist, I have seen my clients suffer from ill-equipped parents, which leads them to feel ill-equipped. When they realize we are all doing the best we are able to do, it is easier to forgive and let go of pain from the past.

A 68-year-old female client, as a six-year-old, behaved violently toward her mother. For sixty years, my client believed she was a terrible person. In a hypnosis session, we discerned that her home environment was chaotic, and her mother lacked the parenting skills to help the child feel heard. After releasing guilt and shame, a few days after our session, for the first time in her life, my client felt an overwhelming sense of self- love.

Changing Your Life from the Inside Out

Can you sense how these concepts can change your life from the inside? As we all learn to lead from within, from our Souls, I envision emotional and spiritual freedom for the world.

Thank you for journeying with
me. I love you!

··· ABOUT DANI GREEN

Dani Green is a certified hypnotherapist, speaker, author, educator, and spiritual advocate. Her passion is guiding clients to rewrite their past, present, and future Story at the subconscious level and to discover their transformative Infinite Greatness. Clients realize Inner Mantras and find power, peace, and a new higher level of consciousness. Dani helps clients find emotional relief, spiritual freedom, improved relationships, health, and business success. Releasing life-draining emotions and becoming aware of their Soul Power is essential to well-being in any area of life. A client went from "I don't want to want to die" to "I have done a mental 180. I have so much more truth and wisdom to empower me day to day." As the owner of Higher Path Healing, Dani meets clients one-on-one, in group sessions, in person, or online. Dani offers a 12-session course called The Soul Power Experience and six-session courses, Be ~~Smoke~~ Free and One & D.O.N.E. Weight Release. She also offers Intuitive Hypnotherapy sessions. Dani opened her hypnotherapy practice in 2015 and uses client-centered hypnotherapy, as well as The Emotion Code, PSYCH-K, and R.I.M. As an Ordained Minister and owner of Celebrations of Life, Dani writes and officiates Weddings and Funerals. Dani has a B.A. from Seattle Pacific University and was a denominational church staff pastor for 14 years. Dani and Kevin have three married children and two adorable grandsons!

Website: www.danigreen.today

Instagram: https://www.instagram.com/danigreen.today/

YouTube: https://www.youtube.com/@SoultoSoulwithDani/about

Facebook/Higher Path Healing: https://www.facebook.com/ActivateYourSoulPower/

Facebook/Celebrations of Life: https://www.facebook.com/danigreen.today/

8 ··· THE OCEAN IS CALLING

ME

by Tina Tesch-Myers

I was born in Australia to German parents as the first generation. My family life was ruled with a strong sense of respect, discipline and love. My brothers were very dominant in my life, especially my twin brother Andreas. I grew up with two amazing brothers who were exceptionally gifted in their own fields. Let's say it was daunting and very difficult for an only girl.

Michael is extremely intelligent and very humble in his demeanor about his brilliance. He is always carefree, honest to his core, and has a smile on his face with a definite, strong, and determined walk and presence. He always brought me down to earth, grounded me, and encouraged me to look at life differently with honest eyes. Michael was always the essence of truth and respect for me. My twin brother, Andreas, who is incredibly gifted with creating phenomenal works of art, never ceases to amaze me as he produces the most amazing and unique pieces. Even at a young age of five, his paintings and drawings were disqualified because the judges couldn't fathom someone at his age could produce such stunning works of art. He was gifted with the vision of seeing everything in three dimensions, so his paintings and drawings would come to life.

Being a twin, I was constantly compared to Andreas and my older brother Michael. I remember very clearly one day when we had family friends over, they had commented on the brilliance of my brothers.

"What can Tina do?" they then asked.

There was silence from my parents.

So, after my duty of serving coffee and cake, I gave them *my* answer.

"Tina is Tina. What you see is what you get."

Then I departed smartly to my safety zone—the beach—because I knew that opening my mouth was not accepted. I always felt so insignificant in my house. Coming from a very strong German upbringing, "the girl is to be seen but not heard." At that time, it frustrated me deeply, and I felt that I was only good as a servant in our household. Now I am so grateful because it only made me determined and strong-willed on the inside. I had to listen to myself and trust that I was making the right decision for my life and my personal journey.

Walking on the beach always brought me out of my insecurities. The vastness of the golden sand that was firm under my feet grounded me instantly. The smell of the ocean is sweet, clean and fresh. It makes me feel so amazingly alive and so grateful to be here on this earth. Then the sound and sight of the ocean are so rhythmic that they lure me in. I watch the waves roll in with ease and grace. Then, on their final journey, they lay themselves out in front of my feet with the remaining energy of the wave, in its white foam that dissolves into the sand. All I wanted was to be submerged and play in the water, where all my insecurities dissolved.

Since I was born, I have been incredibly tenacious, fearless, and loved water in every form. When we had our holidays at Cape Patterson, I turned to the sea for everything. Just being near it would always unearth my greatest passion. An incredible home with endless possibilities for finding my inner answers. I excelled physically in the water. It was my safety zone. It suited my soul, made me feel indestructible, and gave me strength and power that I could not find anywhere else. I knew I could achieve anything. I put my mind to it, against all odds; this would lead me to my deep understanding of what I had to do next.

It was so clear to me that my intuition guided me continuously when I was near the ocean. Just smelling it and being there always calmed my mind and relaxed my soul, and I would be given unexpected answers to problems that were a burden on me. Many times, my answers didn't resonate with my family. My brothers would roll their eyes and not say anything, and my mother would desperately want to change my mind and redirect me to be a sensible young lady to follow her German heritage and upbringing. At times, that certainly didn't resonate with my deep feelings about what I had to do to go forward on my life's path.

I had to listen to my deep feelings and follow what was true for me. With the ocean being my backbone of strength, I had to learn to walk with fear. Turning my fear into courage led me to study in Europe, travel through Africa, to climb the Himalayan mountains, and end up studying in America. I am incredibly grateful for my Germanic upbringing because, at its core, discipline laid an amazing foundation for me. Discipline is my bridge between thought and accomplishment. Add to this my deep sense that I have to be courageous and walk with fear to create a path of change. These played an important role in my life; they always kept me on my toes, so I made fear my companion because it would never go away.

When I made up my mind, I made sure that fear was behind me and courageous discipline was next to me. There are times when fear will sneak up next to me and command too much control, throwing me into chaos. All of my doubts and insecurities would start to dominate my mind and take control of me. I knew deep down I had to follow my purpose, and so I used fear with courageous discipline to push me out of my comfort zone. I respect fear like I respect the ocean; the undertow, currents, and rips all flow together and, at times, are very unseen. It's like going into uncharted waters. I know what I have to do and am willing to take a leap of faith and just do it.

One day, I was walking on my favorite beach in Australia, Cape Paterson, with my amazing son Joaquin, who was fourteen at the time. He gave me some insight that day that I will never forget.

"You guys [my generation] have screwed up the environment, and now we [his generation] have to clean it up."

I stopped and looked into Joaquín's eyes.

"Let's not wait for your generation to take on this responsibility," I said. "We can start to make a difference for the oceans now before it becomes such a huge issue."

Whenever I am near the ocean, I know that my deep feelings about protecting her are ignited inside of me. I must admit, I did run in the opposite direction at first. This mission was terrifying for me and overloaded my senses. The idea of raising global awareness of the complex injustices in our oceans was too expansive and overwhelming for me to even consider.

At first, my self-worth was nowhere to be found. I couldn't fathom that I could achieve anything remotely substantial that would cause even a ripple effect to help the oceans. So instead, I wanted to look in the opposite direction, because I doubted that I was courageous enough to step out and stand up for something I believed in so deeply with every inch of my heart and soul. I wanted to play it safe and not commit to such an overwhelming cause that absolutely terrified me and, at times, made me want to puke in my mouth. All of my fears and insecurities surfaced, and so I attempted to push this deep desire to help the oceans aside. My mind would play out scenarios where I could firmly push everything away in a small and powerful box. To be opened on another day that would conveniently be sometime in the future. So many different stories played out in my mind.

Let someone more gifted with accreditations who would be acknowledged as a superior leader in leading such a monumental quest step forward, I thought. *Someone who was a more capable person. Perhaps even an organization.*

And so, I began to talk myself out of following my passion, convincing myself that it was "too monumental." I would make up stories and talk myself into a false sense of security with a belief system that would give me a feeling of false peace that would dominate my mind. My heart and soul would cringe with a sour taste in my mouth that would linger; this was my truth serum coming to the surface. I felt this deep pit of despair and dishonesty run through my soul, and my voice of truth was squashed. Then an article would fall into my lap, prompting me once again. A video or a message would slap me in the face and make me reflect on *why* I was born and *where* my true passion was—a passion that supports my growth as a human being. With fear as my companion, I finally subdued all those feelings of frustration and incompetence and took a long, hard look at myself in the mirror.

"What are you running away from?" I asked.

I thought about how the ocean was my second home—a place that gave me so much comfort, support, and a deep sense of security. Even today, I thrive in the sensations of being submerged under the water, opening my eyes to look around and see a breathtakingly beautiful beach. When the waves crash down and the surf pounds in, it throws my body into a spin cycle, where I surrender and allow the rhythm of the sea to take me on a wild journey. My body and the water become one, and I trust and know that I will surface again for a breath of fresh air.

This majestic sea needs our attention in so many ways. Deep in my heart and core, I know what I must do to really stretch myself and be a voice for the oceans. Who I must become to have an impact on humanity and this planet. The ocean has its own life force, and she can be incredibly gentle and then ferocious. That is why we must respect this incredible body of water, whose wisdom and strength we cannot misjudge.

She is the pulse of the planet and covers seventy percent of it. I do not believe it is a coincidence that our bodies are also made up of seventy percent water, we have so much in common with the oceans. We have two magnificent lungs and so does our planet—one is green and the other is blue. Our land (the green lung) filled with vegetation and trees, provides twenty percent of our oxygen, whereas the oceans (the blue lung) give us eighty percent. But our oceans are becoming suffocated with plastic.

It makes me cry when I see the mountains of plastic all around us. All you have to do is go into a supermarket and see the vast pallets of plastic bottled water, washing detergents, creams, milk, yogurt, and the list goes on. I look at these, knowing they will either go into the ocean or landfills. We are using the land and the sea as a filtering and dumping system. So many of us have adopted an "out of sight, out of mind" mentality, or "it's not my responsibility; let someone else take care of it." I've even been told with a shrug of the shoulder that they will not be around to see what happens, so they don't care. We truly only recycle a tiny amount, and we are never told the truth of where it all goes.

Plastic is so pervasive in our society that the endless amounts really scare me. There seems to be no stopping at the mounds of products that are made with plastic. People have the misconception that when something is BPA-free, it is harmless, and they can store their water or food in it. However, studies show that certain chemicals in plastic can leach out of the plastic and into the food and beverages we eat and have been linked to health problems such as metabolic disorders and reduced fertility. Harvard Health says this leaching can occur even faster and to a greater degree when the plastic is exposed to heat, such as using Tupperware to reheat your food.

For me personally, I have always hated the smell of Tupperware. I remember the day my mother came home from a Tupperware party with a big round Tupperware container that she could put a cake in. I asked Mum what this hard stuff was called, and she told me in her strong German accent that it's called Tupperware and from America. I spoke out and said it smelled awful and asked if we had to use it. Her response was that we will use it, and you can wash out that smell. To this day, I personally have never bought a Tupperware container, and when I had to clear out our kitchen in my parents' home in Melbourne, I made sure that many of these Tupperware items never made it to our beach house in Cape Paterson. It never ceases to amaze me that people still buy it and say with profound belief that it is "non-toxic."

My passion is to raise public awareness, little by little, to the dangers of plastic use. Oceans are so important to me for the health of humanity and for the future generations that will inherit this earth. We have so many amazing organizations that are helping the oceans: Oceans4Oceans, Ocean Conservancy, Oceana, Bahamas Plastic Movement, and Gyres, to name just a few. They are helping in such a great way, and I am profoundly grateful that we can, together, save our oceans.

My foundation, Move Me, provides educations at the grass roots of the home, to improve family health and wellness. I start at the source of where plastic comes into our home and share how to reduce the consumption of plastic in simple and easy ways. Small changes that we make daily will affect the health of our families, as well as the health of this magnificent planet … all by simply reducing our plastic consumption. We can do this by making changes to the shampoos, conditioners and creams we put on our bodies, as well as the food we buy, how we store and heat it, and the utensils we use daily. In addition to the overuse of plastic, many products on the market have byproducts that become stored in our cells. This movement begins by becoming aware of the hidden toxins in plastic that are affecting our homes and our beautiful oceans. As each of us educates ourselves on how we can make better choices, we will make a wave of difference for our oceans.

Mankind is so overwhelmed with life that the thought of changing anything automatically shifts our minds into rejection, with not another thing that I have to add to my monumentally busy life. The brake pedal is applied, and everything is shifted into the back of the brain. "Another day, I will start when it is more convenient." We personally cannot fathom that small shifts or adjustments can result in mammoth changes to our health or even influence the oceans.

Together, let's add to your quality of life so that you don't have to sacrifice the things that they value or love. Let's open our eyes with a different lens to create a new sense of ease and grace that goes into our minds, bodies and souls. I am passionate about what I do, and the best way I feel that I can contribute my talents to helping the oceans and amazing human beings is with small daily changes in our habits, which would take less than fifteen minutes a day. We can do it!

The ripple effect is incredibly powerful, and when we all work together, we can make a massive change. We cannot solve all our oceans' problems, but we can contribute to moving towards a cure.

⋯ ABOUT TINA TESCH MYERS

Born in vibrant landscapes of Australia to German immigrants, I embarked on a journey that has been as diverse as it has been enriching. My early years were marked by deep curiosity about the world and a passion for understanding the intricacies of what makes life beautiful. My quest for knowledge and beauty led me to study Hotel Management and Catering, where I learned the joy of creating welcoming spaces. However, my creative spirit yearned for more tactile expressions, which I found in the art of woodturning and fine woodworking. Tasmania, with its rich tradition of craftsmanship and its breathtaking natural beauty, became my workshop and inspiration. There, I not only honed my skills but also had the privilege of teaching at Hobart University, sharing my passion and knowledge with eager minds. My journey didn't stop with wood. I've always believed the holistic approach to wellness, which led me to the shores of America. There, delved deep into the study and practice of Rolfing, Visceral Manipulation and Nutrition. These disciplines allowed me to explore the profound connections between body, mind and spirit, and how nurturing each aspect can lead to a balanced and fulfilled life. In 2023, I founded "Move Me," a movement dedicated to enhancing people's health and their home environments. We champion the idea that living in balance and grace can bring inner freedom, not just on an individual level, but also globally. My vision extends to the world around us, particularly our oceans. I am a staunch advocate for a world where our oceans thrive, free from the scourge plastic pollution. Through "Move Me," I aim to inspire others to take plastic-free steps towards a healthier planet.

Website: *www.Move-me.org*
Email: *tinarolfer@gmail.com*
Facebook Business Page: *The Ripple Club Private Club*
Facebook Business Page: *Move Me*
Linkedin: *linkedin.com/tinatesch-myers*

9 ··· BLANK RUNE

by Karen Vaile

I drew the blank rune, Odin's rune. Trust your intuition.
Change is inevitable. Faith in the unknowable. For me, I
always envisioned hitting a wall and just turning left into
that unknown.

As I embark on this reflective journey, tracing the contours of my life and career, I am reminded of the profound impact of intuition and the courage to embrace the unknown. This narrative, inspired by the essence of *She Leads from Within: Intuitive Thought Leadership is Changing the Way Women Do Business*, is not just my story, but a testament to the transformative power of leading from within. It began with a simple yet symbolic act of drawing a blank rune, an act that would unexpectedly guide my entire journey.

This story is about more than personal growth; it's about how intuitive leadership can reshape the way women engage in the world of business, fostering a culture of empowerment, healing and purpose. As we delve into this tale, remember that it's in the uncharted territories of our lives where the most significant transformations occur, guided by the unseen force of our inner wisdom.

As a young person, I grappled with feelings of hurt, confusion and anger. A victim of child sexual abuse, the prevailing belief then was to act as if nothing had happened, based on the assumption that I was too young to remember. This was far from true. Sadly, I became part of a disturbing statistic, experiencing multiple sexual abuses before I even turned eighteen. This left me feeling isolated and alone, burdened with self-hatred. I struggled to make sense of these experiences, often wrongly blaming myself and questioning what I might have done to deserve them. Overwhelmed with emotional pain, I turned to physical pain, which seemed more manageable. Unbeknownst to me at the time, this was self-injurious behavior. In moments of distress, I would hurt myself, like burning my hands on our electric stove or hitting my feet with a mallet, seeking some form of temporary relief from the emotional agony I was enduring. That relief was always just temporary.

During my teenage years, I was on a quest to understand my experiences and feelings. This journey of discovery led me to the second-hand bookstores in my neighborhood. It was there, amidst the labyrinth of bookshelves, I began to perceive a bigger picture and realized that my life had more meaning beyond mere survival. This realization ignited a thirst in me to find that deeper meaning, instinctively knowing it was key to becoming whole and feeling complete. I spent countless hours immersed in ancient texts, searching for answers to the fundamental questions of life and exploring my emerging sense of spirituality.

Questions like, "Is there a God?" and, "What does spirituality mean to me?" occupied my thoughts. This fascination soon led me into the realms of the occult and divination, where I experimented with I Ching, Tarot cards, and Totem Animals, among others. Little did I know, these explorations were the first steps on a path that would shape my life's philosophy and career, embodying the spirit of intuitive leadership that I would come to champion.

During one of my explorations in these bookstores, I discovered *The Book of Runes*. Intrigued, I tried my hand at drawing a rune and pulled out the blank rune. Its origin is a topic of debate among enthusiasts—some say it's an original part of the rune set, while others believe it was added later. The blank rune represents "The Unknowable" —it symbolizes both an end and a beginning, like the cycle of death and birth. It beckons one to jump the void into the unknown. A leap of faith and an act of courage. In my life, I've likened this to facing a daunting, pitch-black wall, akin to the eerie darkness of a Halloween haunted house. Faced with this, what could one do but boldly turn left, stepping into the uncharted and continuing forward?

Embracing the unknown and following my intuition has been my compass, guiding me through life's labyrinth. It's about trusting that instinctive turn left when faced with daunting challenges and jumping into the void with faith. This approach shaped not only my spiritual journey but also how I celebrated each of life's milestones, seeking deeper meaning in them. The whimsical celebration by my family when my second breast finally made an appearance at fifteen was more than a quirky tradition; it represented my initial steps into the complex world of adulthood. Then came my twentieth birthday, a poignant marker I never imagined reaching, symbolizing both a victory over early struggles and the threshold to a new life phase.

As I journeyed through the shared societal milestones, like the reflective thirties and the transformative forties, these weren't merely chronological markers. They were pivotal moments of introspection and decision-making, echoing the spiritual exploration of my youth. In these decades, often characterized by a period of reassessment or transformation, I found opportunities for profound personal growth, contemplating the past and envisaging the future as I navigated the evolving landscape of relationships, careers, and self-identity.

Unlike many of my peers who struggled with the empty nest syndrome after their children left home, I didn't have children to redefine my life around. Yet, in my forties, I was engulfed by a deep sense of unhappiness and dissatisfaction. Over the years, I had diligently developed my skills and carved a career path for myself, eventually rising to a leadership role as Supervisor in a youth-serving agency. Alongside my job, I earned a diploma and furthered my education with a postgraduate certificate in advanced counselling. Despite these achievements, I found myself at a standstill, unable to advance further without more education. This feeling of being stuck was accompanied by a growing fear. I worried about becoming significantly older than my clients and staff, feeling the generational divide expanding. It became clear to me that it was time to move on, to seek new paths and opportunities.

Deciding to end my career felt like coming full circle, back to the beginning. I remember in my teenage years when abuse was not readily acknowledged or talked about, I used to pray to God to send someone to me that I could talk with, who would be there for me. But that person never came. I felt so isolated and confused by the mix of emotions I couldn't understand. This is why, when the chance to volunteer and become an unofficial "Big Sister" to a teenager in a group home presented itself, I seized it. This decision seemed contradictory, especially since just a year earlier, I had dissuaded my best friend from pursuing a career as a Youth Counsellor. Back then, I saw teenagers as "nasty" and "hoodlums" and couldn't fathom why anyone would want to work with them, so I encouraged her to study Addiction Counselling instead.

However, something within me, a quiet intuition barely a whisper, urged me to take this volunteer opportunity. It was like facing another of those metaphorical walls in my life; I simply turned left, not fully understanding my actions or where they would lead. I followed my instincts and with a leap of faith, I embraced the unknown.

These young women were placed in the group home due to their challenging behaviors, which were too difficult to manage in their homes or foster care. I soon realized that this group home was often seen as the last resort for these hard-to-serve clients, typically being a step away from more severe consequences like incarceration or institutionalization. Despite their varied expressions of distress, all these women shared a common experience of childhood sexual abuse. Their actions, though diverse, were all self-destructive responses to their deep-seated pain. I recognized myself in every one of those teenagers.

I quickly found myself applying for a job and advancing through various roles. As I worked with these young women, I discovered a profound truth: the more I helped them, the more I healed myself. Each act of support and time spent with them contributed to my own healing journey. This process was about more than just giving; it was about understanding the essence of true receiving. By aiding these women in confronting their own struggles, I simultaneously addressed the wounds of my own troubled years, which were marked by depression and suicidal thoughts. In helping them to understand what had happened and seeing how they were not to blame, I freed myself from that deep shame I carried. I started to understand and embrace the word survivor, leaving the victim behind.

This path of healing and discovery taught me the value of trusting my instincts, even when the future seemed uncertain. Embracing the unknown became a crucial part of my journey. The inner turmoil I once felt, like a knot in my stomach, was gradually replaced by a burning passion and a clear sense of direction. This newfound purpose not only healed me but also helped me find my true self.

However, as time passed, I began to feel a growing disconnect, particularly with the younger generation, both the "kids" I was helping and the young staff I managed. I didn't want to reach a point where I'd be out of touch, humorously referred to as "Granny" by others. I saw the need for change before that gap widened irreversibly.

The suggestion of becoming a police officer initially made me cringe. As a liberal feminist for most of my adult life, the idea of joining what I perceived as "those" ranks was far from appealing. In my view, they were the very archetype of power-driven Neanderthals, often exploiting the vulnerabilities of the people I aimed to serve and protect. Yet, the idea lingered in my mind, ticking off several practical boxes. They would fund my education—that was a plus. The pay was good, and the pension was attractive. Importantly, schooling would be accommodated within my work hours. However, the reality of having to carry—and potentially use—a gun weighed heavily on me.

I sought advice from my brother and best friend, deciding that if either of them objected, I would drop the idea of becoming a police officer. To my surprise, both supported the idea. My friend even believed I'd make a good cop, which I wasn't sure how to take, considering her own low regard for the police profession.

Drawing the blank rune seemed symbolic at this juncture. There were several preparations and steps I needed to take before even submitting my resume. Yet, deep within, I sensed a profound truth: this was the next chapter in my life's journey. All it required was faith, trust, and the willingness to turn left when confronted with a wall and do the necessary work.

Taking on this work meant making a firm decision and then following it through with consistent, persistent actions. Every step taken was a move towards the goal I had set for myself. This process is like overcoming an addiction to drugs or alcohol, where every moment is focused on staying clean and sober. Pursuing a goal demands that same level of singular focus, a relentless drive towards completion. In some circles, this is referred to as a spiritual awakening, while others might call it a quantum leap. It's about a deep devotion and commitment, fueled by unwavering drive and momentum.

The word "decision" is intriguing when you think about its roots. "Incision" means to cut into, and "decision" can imply cutting off. When you decide, it means you're fully committed, leaving no room for a Plan B or any alternatives. You cut off all other options. It's like striving for sobriety; you can't be partially clean and sober—you either are or you're not. With this mindset, I resolved to do whatever was necessary to apply for the job, fully dedicating myself to the path I had chosen, spurred on by an intuition.

The driving force that was propelling me towards my career path was marked by a profound and personal tragedy—the murder of my best friend at the hands of her own husband. This heartbreaking incident had left me with a deep sense of regret; a feeling that, somehow, I should have been able to prevent her fate. It was the pivotal moment in my life that intensified my resolve to help other women. The sensation in my stomach, which I came to recognize as my calling, was urging me to action.

Ever since my early twenties, as an Employee Assistance Representative, I had felt a mission to support and empower women. Having faced my own traumas, I understood that in helping others heal, I could find healing for myself too. This drive led me to a keen interest in Sex Crimes, where I could make a significant impact. Inspired by Detective Olivia Benson from *Law and Order,* I saw a reflection of the advocate I wanted to become. What began as a hopeful idea had now turned into a burning desire.

With intense focus and determination, I committed to this path, echoing Alexander the Great's resolve when he burned his ships upon reaching enemy territory—a symbol of total commitment. I was going all in, dedicating myself to a cause that was not only deeply personal but also a means to heal both myself and others.

The entire process was expected to take about a year. During this time, I grappled with the idea of carrying a gun as part of my equipment and being prepared to use it if needed. This was a significant challenge for me, as I had always been against guns. Additionally, I needed to prepare for the required tests that are part of the application process, including improving my physical fitness.

I approached the Physical Readiness Evaluation for Police (PREP test) with confidence, believing it would be a breeze. After all, I had run multiple marathons and recently progressed to triathlons. To me, a half-marathon was "just a half," seemingly effortless, almost like a leisurely walk in the park. However, this confidence quickly dissipated during the test. As I ran around the gym, climbing stairs, leaping over walls, and maneuvering weight simulators, I struggled immensely. Lifting and dragging a 150-pound dummy for fifteen meters proved to be especially challenging. The shuttle run, which required progressively faster sprints, was another hurdle. Despite completing all tasks, which was more than most women there could manage, I fell short of the required completion times. I left the gym that day in tears, feeling utterly defeated.

In the days following my setback, I was nursing not just my physical wounds but also my bruised ego and the fragments of my dreams. *Where had my passion and burning desire gone? What about that guiding intuition and life's purpose?* I wallowed in these thoughts, but the feeling that I was being driven in a specific direction remained unshakable. I was convinced that this path was meant for me. I began to question what more I needed to do to succeed.

Soon, I found myself doing push-ups every hour, stretching my limits. Each morning, I ran laps around the high school track, practicing the shuttle run over and over. My determination and drive were unwavering. People around me wondered why I persisted, despite the difficulties. They suggested that these obstacles might be a sign that this path wasn't meant for me. But I didn't see it that way. My intuition urged me to dig deeper and lean into the challenge.

A year after deciding to pursue a policing career, I submitted my resume to the Headquarters. Remarkably, less than five hours later, I received a call from the employment office inviting me for an interview. In that moment, I knew for certain that this was my path and the only way for me was forward. But it wasn't a straightforward journey. I stood out among the recruits: I was a generation older, gay in a predominantly straight group, in a long-term relationship when most of them came from broken homes, and a vegan, in stark contrast to the average candidate. These differences made the path challenging, yet immensely rewarding. Now, I go to work each day with one guiding question: how can I be of service? And, every day, I have the opportunity to live out that purpose.

As my policing career reaches its twilight, I find myself pondering, *Where can I be of service next?* When a friend suggested coaching, it resonated deeply with that small, inner voice which had always guided me through the unknown. It was an enthusiastic "yes!" that marked the beginning of a new journey. This path, blending my twenty years of counseling experience with skills honed as an emergency responder, uniquely positions me to empower women in ways I hadn't imagined before.

Now, having healed from my past traumas, I dedicate myself to helping women find their freedom—freedom from guilt, obligations and regrets, and the freedom to prioritize themselves. This journey is not just about thriving and self-reliance; it's about inspiring others. And in the process of giving, I've received immeasurably—forgiveness, healing and a renewed sense of purpose.

My focus in coaching is on building Confidence, enhancing Communication, and fostering Connections. Each step forward is a testament to the power of embracing the unknown, trusting that inner voice, and taking that intuitive leap into a future filled with possibilities.

Reflecting on my journey, particularly the moment I drew the blank rune, I see a vivid reflection of the themes in this book. This experience, guided by intuition and an openness to the unknown, has shown the transformative power of leading from within. The blank rune, a symbol of both endings and beginnings, has been a beacon in trusting the unseen and tapping into the strength of intuition. It has revealed that true leadership and courage are born from venturing into uncharted territories, guided by our inner wisdom.

Continuing this path, I've come to understand a universal truth: leading with intuition is not merely a personal transformation, it's a revolutionary approach to business and leadership. This journey of embracing the unknown, as the blank rune suggests, transcends personal growth. It's about fostering a life filled with purpose, healing and empowerment, and extends to inspiring change and innovation in business and the wider community.

In helping others, I've experienced profound healing. The act of giving has been a journey of receiving in ways I never anticipated. It's a cycle of growth and empowerment that enriches both the giver and the receiver. My story is a testament to the idea that when we lead from within, guided by intuition, we don't just transform ourselves; we pave the way for a new era of intuitive and thoughtful leadership in business and beyond.

⋯ ABOUT KAREN VAILE

Karen Vaile's journey as a Life and Mindset Coach is a compelling narrative of empowering women to lead with confidence, intuition and resilience. Her life's work is a testament to her unwavering commitment to fostering freedom and self-belief in women. Starting her mission as an Employee and Family Assistance Program (EFAP) representative, Karen made significant strides in combating domestic violence. She went above and beyond, using her home as a refuge for women in need, symbolizing her dedication to emotional, physical and spiritual freedom. It set the foundation for her lifelong dedication to empowering women, a theme that has resonated through her subsequent roles and personal journey. Karen's transition from a Youth & Family Counselor to a Residential Supervisor marked a crucial phase in her career, intensifying her focus on empowerment. She discovered the transformative power of letting go, trusting in oneself, and the importance of faith, which later became central themes in her coaching philosophy. Karen's time as a 911 responder as a police officer was a period of profound professional growth. She learned to navigate crises with decisive action and clear communication, developing an acute understanding of the human condition. These high-pressure experiences were instrumental in her ability to build trust and rapport swiftly, essential tools in her mission to empower women, teaching them not only to survive but to thrive in the face of life's unpredictability. Through her mentoring work, Karen imparts these lessons, helping women to recognize their worth, reclaim their lives, and unlock their true potential. Her coaching and mentoring, enriched by her personal experiences, have been vital in helping women embrace their full potential.

Website: *https://www.karenscoachingkorner.com*
Facebook: *https://www.facebook.com/karenvaile2*
Facebook Business Page: *https://www.facebook.com/karenscoachingkorner*
LinkedIn: *https://www.linkedin.com/in/karen-vaile-coaching*
Instagram: *https://www.instagram.com/karens_coaching_korner*

10 ··· TRUE SURRENDER: ESCAPING MY OWN CAGE

by Sylvie Stuart

Five weeks before our wedding, I was given a stage four cancer diagnosis. Lymph nodes noticeably swelled around my neck, changing the face I knew to be mine. Plans around a honeymoon celebration were now shifted to discussions on if there would even be a wedding. Fear took root on how long I would be around. The whirlwind of emotions was overwhelming. There was a weighted darkness over this time of celebration that we didn't know how to get out from under.

How do we tell everyone?

I laid in bed for a few days wondering how I got there. I had been more tired than usual, but that had been easily explained by my to-do lists, and nothing an extra pot of coffee couldn't fix. I became afraid of my body while buried under the covers. I felt like I had failed my fiancé, was terrified of being a burden, and couldn't figure out where I made a wrong turn with my health.

Towards the end of the second day, while still in bed, I heard a loud voice.

"It'll all be okay," it said.

It was unrecognizable. I had no idea where it came from and still somehow, in that moment, believed those words. They ended up becoming an anchor of guidance over the next decade. Despite my inner being feeling paralyzed, there was an assuredness and authoritative aspect to this voice that shook me out of bed.

We had our wedding, and over the following few weeks we met in oncologist offices with notepaper and determined attitudes. These meetings left my husband and I feeling both defeated and pessimistic about my future, which went directly against our belief in the power of the mind. They started unleashing doubt and draining hope. The type of cancer I had wasn't normally seen in women of my young age, so we were grasping at straws on how to treat it. The options presented were the "we hope this works" options.

One overcast afternoon as we sat in our black Honda in the hospital parking lot with bloodshot eyes, we posed a new question.

"Do I *have* to get treatment?"

We were constantly having to rebuild emotionally after each meeting because we still wanted to have children of our own. The life we dreamed hadn't even gotten off the runway. Since we didn't have a convincing conventional treatment option, maybe we could heal and support my body a different way. Doing natural treatments was the scariest decision I have ever made and despite the arguments we received from family and friends, that convicted, unknown voice kept running through my mind stronger than any other.

"It'll all be okay."

Veering from the traditional treatment plan put the strategy on our shoulders. Anxiety built as I tried to solve this "life or death" puzzle with no prior training. I felt extremely underqualified and out of my league. My husband even came home from work one day to find me crying on the couch. I hadn't eaten all day, because I was so frightened of feeding the cancer, and I couldn't move. He gently hugged me and let me know I just needed to nourish myself in that moment.

Over the next several years, we traveled to different doctors to detox and boost my immune system. I went vegetarian, then vegan, then fully raw. I spent many hours every day doing infrared saunas, IVs, colonics, coffee enemas, juicing, preparing organic food, grounding, meditating and receiving bodywork.

Three years later, I got strong enough to give birth to our beautiful healthy daughter, which is my biggest life accomplishment. I went to seminars, read books, listened to podcasts, faced fears, journaled and continued working in our real estate business.

A few years into this uber-structured regimen, I had a huge realization. This was a *lot* of effort to continue daily, I was exhausted and doubting I could keep this pace indefinitely. My life had become so regimented and inflexible that I felt like I was only living for the treatments and depriving myself of so much. I was afraid to interact with friends and the fun parts of life in fear it would be devastating on my immune system. I realized I was controlling my external life, but maybe there was an internal emotional component that I wasn't accessing.

How do I get to that?

I had to continue focus on myself in my desperate attempt to heal and unfortunately my relationships suffered. Most painfully, my marriage almost didn't survive. In perpetual survival mode, I just hadn't seen another way. I kept hearing, "kick cancer's ass," "fighter," and "warrior," yet it started to feel counterintuitive. The cancer itself was mutated versions of my own cells. Deep down those words felt abandoning to my soul, even if it was a piece I wanted to reverse. I started to see my disease as a teacher.

What if, years ago, I had been forcing my body out of health by focusing on how many of my to-dos I could cross off and the results of my real estate business? What if there was an emotional/spiritual component missing that I wasn't connecting with because I was distracting myself by being so regimented? What if that structure was an illusion of control? What if I needed to surrender to this disease? And not surrender in a way that gave it power over me, but out of resistance and into acceptance?

Still, how do I go about this?

The whispers were coming.

I continued finding more modalities and treatments to "heal" my body including more obligations and rules to follow for myself, making my daily box smaller and smaller. Any kind of spirituality was an afterthought, and seemed like a luxury I couldn't afford to give any time to. I would add it to my list once I got better. I was disciplined to an elite degree to everything outside of me, yet I had little awareness on what was going on inside. My disease sat in waiting, ready to pounce harder.

I got pregnant again and had a miscarriage that landed me in the ER twice from excessive bleeding and then emergency surgery, reminding me I was still at the mercy of this illness. Despite all my efforts, I couldn't relax and enjoy any of the healing I was trying to achieve, because it needed such constant attention. Little did we know, time was closing in.

Our hearts were filled a few years later when we adopted our precious baby boy. What was previously a ginormous hole and strain on us as a couple, was filled instantly by the joyous sounds of his constant belly-laughter. What a magical being he still is. He truly brought a new sense of hope to our family when we needed it most.

Shortly after, I got COVID. My body handled it better than anticipated but left me exhausted, and I lost the ground I had gained over the previous decade of extreme obedience and discipline to my health. My lymph nodes swelled up even more and this time with extreme pain—I couldn't turn my head or lay down without going into excruciating spasm. For over a month I could only sit and sleep in a recliner. I was losing weight, gasping for air and yet I was still determined to find a way to get through it. I had other episodes over the years of mind-twisting health situations, but we had always found a way to support my body through it. I thought that I could surely figure this out, however, I was unaware my ego was still driving me down a dark path.

Barely surviving on my recliner, I went to a healer to move the pain. She stared at me in disbelief and insisted I go to the ER again immediately. I was shocked and unsure of the urgency. My pain was beyond a ten, and yet I couldn't see I needed more help. Luckily, my husband immediately drove me to the hospital. Hunched over, I slowly shuffled through the doors, and the minute they took my oxygen levels, they had me in a wheelchair off to a private room to take images. I had three liters of strep pneumonia pressing on my right lung and was twenty-four hours from organ failure. I was so out of it from the pain that I couldn't quite understand everything that was happening.

Apparently, I was talking to people who weren't there, potentially discussing the changes I would need to make if I were to survive.

The strep tissue was unusually dense so they pushed a tube through my back, which made being stuck in bed agonizing. After they drained enough liquid, they performed a life-saving lung surgery with three more big tubes coming out of my right ribcage.

My husband and I spent our ten-year wedding anniversary in that hospital, once again canceling our plans. I felt utterly defeated. I was trying everything I could to think positively. I had done everything "right" for years, lived this life of deprivation and now our celebration of making it this far in our marriage was taken from us too? I was furious and out of motivation. I didn't know what else I needed to learn from this "teacher," and I was devastated. When I got home from the hospital, I had to stay on oxygen, muddle around with a walker and at only forty-four, was skin and bones.

The news from the surgery was the cancer was deep in the tissue they removed, I was now out of options and had to do traditional treatment. Something beyond me was keeping my body alive at this point. I was physically weaker than I had been my entire life. I was too weak and hurting to pick up or hug my children, and tried to keep a happy face when they would ask to snuggle. Back in my recliner, I felt like my soul was broken and felt crushed by the weight of massive amounts of shame.

Inside, I was screaming from a place of emptiness.

I have two little kids who need me—how could I sit in a chair suffering immensely up until the very brink of death? Was I *that* stubborn? Was it *that* hard for me to ask for and receive help? What was I missing?

I cried for a full day, staring at this aspect of my "shadow" with all new clarity. Exhausted, and with nowhere else to go, I started to let go a little bit more. I had been on this journey for so long, and even though my ego and identity had become a part of it, all of this was starting to crumble. I couldn't steady myself and I was falling. I closed my eyes and saw a clear vision of me standing in full body armor holding a shield and a sword. A tall, skinny, bright Being told me it was time to surrender. Reluctantly, I put my shield and sword down and stood back up, chin in the air, as if to say "there, I have surrendered."

The Being shook its head.

"My love, if you think surrender is standing there in a full suit of armor, you don't yet understand," it said.

I was speechless and angry.

I am surrendering! I thought. *What else do you want from me? I've given everything!*

I looked down and my hands were in fists.

There was a message here that I would soon receive.

I began walking outside, starting small and making a goal each day to go a little further. I was stunned that the trees, bushes and grasses all started popping out energetically, almost as if the rest of the world was muted and only nature was there, reaching for me. It was crystal clear, consuming all my senses. Houses and sidewalks just disappeared. I could feel the individual personalities of nature. I tripped a few times because my eyes were glued to everything green that I passed. I had never experienced this magic before and didn't know how long it would last. It felt so nourishing and supportive that I wanted to soak up any and all of that energy.

Have these energies been here the entire time waiting for me to see them?

As I walked with them, I saw them coaxing me to wake up, pulling my soul to the surface, commanding deep eye contact and showing me the beauty of letting go and expanding. I was in a four-dimensional wonderland, and in these moments, I was invincible! I started slipping between the cracks of reality and dimension. I was feeling and seeing God for the first time in my life and this was so much different than I had imagined.

Looking back, I see that God had been a shepherd and the voice that comforted me all these years. Gracefully allowing me to follow what I thought was best, placing boundaries to bounce off to continue me down the right path. Giving soft messages over and over again, and if needed and unheeded, turning up the volume over time.

Emotional Freedom Technique (EFT, or "tapping") was one of those messages that was introduced to me softly a few times before I was ready to pay attention. It was time to dive inward in a deliberate effort to fully surrender and EFT was there to catch me. I started to feel emotional patterns I didn't even know existed shift with total acceptance. It helped me process countless life traumas I had buried inside. I discovered I had stuffed immeasurable grief and anger deep down in my body around losing my father suddenly twenty-five years earlier at a time when I still desperately needed his guidance. He was a minister who had done everything for others, and I had felt abandoned and punished by God. I had retreated and turned my back on him.

That loss immobilized me in all aspects of my life for decades. Tears were always right behind my eyes at the very mention of my father, and no matter how much work I did on it, time wasn't healing that wound. What I thought I had processed was just numbing my feelings, and they were frozen in my body.

EFT allowed the energy of these stuck emotions to be acknowledged and moved. I witnessed my grief, guilt, shame, anxiety, anger, resentment and fear be gently swept out from the deepest parts of my existence. I started to see how completely disconnected I had been from my body and how tensely my body and spirit had been holding itself. I had been on this enormous "healing" quest for years and didn't realize I was trying to think and force my way through it. The frequency I emitted of resistance to my disease did not support my healing efforts. My body had been in a five-alarm state, and it just did not feel safe to sink into it and feel it fully.

EFT gave me the loving technique I needed to sit in the areas of my body that hurt, the areas that were in fear, in resistance, and with the memories I had blocked when I was in survival mode as a child and young woman. I started to "see" beyond the vision of my eyes, patterns I had created to feel safe in the world, that were no longer serving me. Instead of going to these spaces and applying guilt for holding on to it for so long or feeling angry that it ever happened in the first place, I was able to sit with "me," hold "me," love "me," and hear what my so had been trying to say for so long.

I then forgave myself.

In these sessions I took off my suit of armor and embraced these emotions like a little child who was hurting. Once this happened, the weight and judgment dissolved. I started to feel more worthy of the love that I had been blocking instead of continuing to starve to death emotionally and spiritually from the custom cage I created for myself. I noticed that when I had shields up, they blocked the good from coming in too. The more I removed my armor, the more I felt worthy and loved by myself and God. I hadn't considered I wasn't letting God in through the shame I felt by holding onto the layers of these stuck emotions, patterns and barriers.

God was always there, waiting for me to allow access.

I started to deeply understand my disease and the loving message it had been trying to show me. I gained so much compassion for my innocent inner child who always felt I could carry the pain for everyone else. I felt powerless and self-doubt when I couldn't ease the suffering of others, and that caused me to distrust my intuition, separating my spirit from my body. My body got so desperate for *my* attention it acted out in a way I could no longer ignore.

Layer by layer, slowly, I shed these areas of resistance.

I started a newer conventional cancer treatment as my last option almost eleven years after my initial diagnosis. I used EFT to show up differently for treatment. That first day in the infusion room, I walked in excited, ready and determined. When fear and anxiety showed up, I would just tap, allowing them to express themselves, inviting them to move through, and they did. Utilizing EFT during this time was magical. It took me out of my preconceived belief of what healing was and put me into a quantum state of healing where anything felt within reach.

I knew the combination of conventional medicine and the energy work I was diving into was allowing my body to truly heal. When I got the news that my bone marrow no longer showed signs of cancer, it only confirmed what I had already known on a vibrational and spiritual level. This process has been more daunting and beautiful than I could have imagined. This complete journey, with all the painful pitfalls along the path, evolved everything within me.

Today, I am more alive!

I am more alive with my kids, husband, family and friends. I am present, awakening all my senses. I still feel nature's energy cheering for me, singing to a deep piece of my soul, like an old friend. I feel Mother Earth pulling energy out that is not meant for me and transmuting it into something that sends more light and love out into the world. I see energy patterns in front of me everywhere I go, and life feels more like a hologram that we have power over to create the life we want for ourselves. I have come to fully see that the life I've been dreaming of—the life that was *meant* for me—is here to fully immerse myself in.

To be able to claim this new life, I must leave behind any and all self-doubt. I must show up—without armor—as my authentic being. My dream life is out of reach if I am in the cage of self-doubt, ego, and have shields up. When I stand in the confidence of my essence, power and truth, it changes everything. I see the emotional patterns in me, and in others. I now feel my strength. *This* is what my disease was trying to teach me. Had I not gone through the gauntlet of unbelievable suffering and fear, I would never have gotten to the point where I was forced to change and let go of my illusion of control.

There's a saying, "Everything you want is outside of your comfort zone." The world is in desperate need for more of us to courageously stand as our authentic selves and interact with each other from this position. So many shifts are happening, we all feel it. What if all that was needed was for the *real* you to show up and that was enough? Whether it's connecting with a higher source, or your higher self, however you see it. Your true power can shift your frequency, your vibration, your effect on the world, and that can shift everything.

My soul calling was to become a Clinical EFT Practitioner. Helping others use EFT has shown me even more the emotional patterns we as humans experience. Instead of feeling alone and separate in the emotions, I connect and share with other people. I have been guided. It's clear to me that feeling energy has been my superpower all along, *not* a weakness. Now I know how to use it in a way that lights my heart on fire.

I am honored to help clients dance with the energy of their emotional cages by meeting them where they're at, in this very moment, with total acceptance. I help others build the framework to increase their joy and confidence so they can go help even more people. I hold space that allows them to discover the inner superpowers they've always had by digging deep into the roots of energy patterns and not just trimming the thorny branches that show up as external reactions we have.

I believe we all came into this world with superpowers.

Some of us got stuck in our story along the way. If you're going through a challenge, consider that it may be a calling to uncover more of who you are. The more people show up in the world operating with the strength and confidence of their superpowers, can literally change our reality. Like a stone thrown in water, each of us could cause a ripple effect of positive and massive change.

⋯ ABOUT SYLVIE STUART

I am a Certified Clinical Emotional Freedom Technique (EFT) Practitioner and Empath Empowerment Guide. I have a deep understanding of what it's like to feel others' energy intensely, as I've experienced it firsthand throughout my life. For the longest time, I viewed my empathic nature as a weakness. It often felt overwhelming and took a toll on my health. I have worked through major losses, childhood trauma, stage four cancer and night terrors, which further deepened my understanding of the complexities of trauma and its effects on our well-being. In my quest for healing and self-realization, I discovered the transformative power of EFT. Through this modality, I gained the tools to shed the layers of emotional pain associated with loss and trauma. EFT became a catalyst for my personal growth and allowed me to reclaim my power, transforming my empathic abilities from a burden into a source of strength. Now, my mission is to guide fellow empaths towards self-empowerment and help them unlock their full potential. I provide a safe and nurturing space for empaths to explore their sensitivity and establish healthy boundaries. With my expertise in Clinical EFT and my personal journey of healing, I offer a holistic approach to empower empaths to serve others while maintaining their own emotional and energetic balance. Together, we'll navigate the complexities of energy sensitivity, uncover your innate strengths for you to make a profound difference in the lives of others. If you're ready to embark on a transformative journey towards self-empowerment and impactful service, I'm here to support you every step of the way.

Website: *TaprootEFT.com*
Instagram: *@TaprootEFT*
Facebook: *https://www.facebook.com/TaprootEFT*
Schedule a Session: *https://TaprootEFT.as.me*
Schedule a Phone Consultation: *https://TaprootEFT.as.me/PhoneConsu*

11 ⋯ MATTERS OF THE HEART

by Melisa Shelton

I grew up in a mostly upper middle class, suburban area. I attended large award-winning public schools, and our dance functions were held at the local country club. I was an only child until age five and didn't attend preschool, so I spent most of my first five years with close family. As you can imagine, my first day of kindergarten was a monumental one. Like with most "first day of kindergarten" experiences, my parents were as anxious and excited as I was for the big day. My mom did my hair, I put on my new outfit, and I rode the bus for the first time. I met my teacher, found my desk, and took in all the colors, toys, noises and other students. I listened carefully to the teacher's words and expectations, and I was obedient.

I came home from school tired and overwhelmed but ready to take on this new adventure. And as any proud and eager mother would, my mom was right there to ask me about my day just as soon as I walked through the door. She wanted to know every detail, and I am sure I had much to say. One comment of mine stood out, however. So much so that she still remembers it to this day.

"Mom, are my shoes Nikes?"

She seemed surprised by my question but was quick to respond.

"They are just like Nikes, honey."

I was satisfied with her response and moved right along, unknowing that that was just the beginning of my heart's journey to knowing, trusting and loving myself; a journey that would conclude in a transformation from the inside out—one that would not only lead me to attract great love, opportunity, friendship and knowledge, but also give me the strength, gratitude, faith and humility to persevere when times would otherwise seem hopeless.

As I did grow up in an affluent area, unlike most of the families that lived in our area, my family lived differently. All my family members on both sides had lived locally for generations. My grandmother owned one of the few remaining lots of acreage that still displayed the small farmhouse, barn and fruit trees that made up my mother's childhood memories. A new trailer had also been built on the property; this is where my grandmother would eventually move to, and where many of my fondest childhood memories would be experienced.

The area that was once like that of my grandmother's property—farm lots of modest family properties with modest family homes—over time had been sold to developers and turned into master planned luxury living communities. The woods where I grew up building forts and ponds where I caught frogs became forbidden property—protected wetlands—guarded from illegal trespassers by cold metal fences.

As a young child I remember being different, feeling more deeply than others seemed to, and struggling with the frequent conflict between my desire to belong and my heart that so often would, without mercy, pull me to not conform. You see, I loved where I grew up, but for different reasons than one might assume. I knew where the frogs liked to hide and what time of day they liked to feed. I knew what time of year they would come out of hibernation and start singing again. I knew the exact path to take in the woods to get to the clearing that made the best play fort and what looked to be the biggest dinosaur footprint ever viewed by mankind. There was also a small pond that I often wondered had ever been discovered, or if it would remain God's and my secret. What may have seemed trite to many was significant to me. Over the course of a week's time, I went from having a sense of connection to my environment—a sense of safety and home and placing my identity in those feelings—to being told that I was none of those things at all. The messaging that I quickly received was that I should be ashamed of those parts of me.

As early as the age of five, after the first day of kindergarten, I began to realize that the world I lived in, although similar in ways, was dramatically different from the world I was seeing others experience around me. I began to feel like *I* was different, like *I* didn't belong. This messaging only continued to sell itself to me as I progressed through young adulthood. I came to factual realizations, such as my friends traveling the world for leisure when my family went camping, and my peers' parents owning vacation homes when my family went on occasional road trips for vacation. Academics also seemed like a losing battle. I knew I wasn't the smartest kid in school and to compete for grades and appear as educated as my peers (especially when it came to group assignments) was quite anxiety-provoking. Many of my peers had parents with college educations, teachers for parents, or received private tutoring outside of school. I had to rely on myself, the copious notes that I desperately took in class each day, and prayer.

The feelings of not belonging were not the worst of the feelings, however. Although I may have been different, and my world dissimilar to many of my peers, I lived a life that I was also very proud of. My parents and grandmothers worked extremely hard to provide absolutely everything for me—every opportunity and material possession they could afford, but so much more. I was not naive to the fact that I was truly richer than so many others, for I also had an endless trust fund at my disposal with the most priceless of all commodities. I had caretakers that believed in me, trusted me, were there to listen and spend quality time with me, and were dependable, loyal and warm. I was genuinely the wealthiest kid I had ever known. However, to live in my head and heart space with the conflicting messages of not belonging and not being enough, despite my gratitude, began to take its toll. Guilt turned into deep shame, and I unknowingly began to question my own sense of self.

Fast forward, as I continued to work hard at achieving to earn my worth through graduate school into young adulthood. I struggled in romantic relationships. Men of high caliber that were likely good for me I would keep at a distance. I put up walls to protect myself because I was too fearful that they only loved me for my superficial qualities, my achievements and my success. All the things I had spent my lifetime thus far working so hard to gain acceptance, ironically, was what I rejected internally. I was afraid that if these men got too close, they would uncover the fraud that I was underneath my makeup and resume, and they would most certainly be disappointed, leaving me to feel once again isolated in a world of billions with nowhere to belong.

To avoid this perceived threat, I chose to give my heart to men who were less deserving of it. Little did I know at the time that one relationship would not only leave me shattered, but the fragments of a soul that remained of me would be so damaged and I would be forced to rebuild myself—by myself—from scratch.

I still vividly remember the first time he raised his voice. We hadn't been dating long when we had our first difference of opinion. I couldn't tell you what the conversation was about; I have zero recollection. What I do remember were his eyes. His eyes opened wide and went from a warm familiar shade of evening sunshine to a dark that I didn't recognize. His voice was deep and loud, but I could no longer understand the words being spoken or their meaning. I could hear my own inner thoughts interjecting, making things even more confusing. It was like time stood still; I felt frozen. I finally was able to get up and walk away, down the hallway from my living room to my bedroom. He followed me. I sat on my bed and cowered; trembling while he stood over me continuing to bellow until his point was made. I am not sure what he was upset about exactly, but I can tell you with confidence that there were fourteen cat hairs on my black Nike yoga pants. I counted them twenty-two times.

He did end up apologizing after my first exposure to his rage. I explained to him that I had never experienced anything of the sort in my life; he shared that yelling, cussing, shaming, emotional abuse and neglect were common occurrences in his upbringing and it had been that way in his family for generations. I was smart enough to see the bright red flags flying but he assured me that he had done work on himself, on healing his past relationships, and on navigating his family dynamics through personal counseling. I decided to give him the benefit of the doubt; after all, his good qualities seemed to outweigh the bad.

Before long, I was welcomed to join his family get-togethers. In the beginning things seemed so positive with high energy; everyone appeared so close to one another. The joking, the laughter, the comradery—it was something I wanted to belong to. I wanted to be accepted by them so much that I said yes to many things that put my partner's needs, and the needs of his family, first and neglected my own. I started to learn that there were many rules and expectations, but most of them were unspoken. It was just assumed that I would navigate these expectations—no heads up, no grace, and certainly no compromise. I eventually discovered there were consequences for not conforming to the patriarch. These were also not discussed and as I unfortunately learned the hard way, even the thought of doing so would be met with denial, which was tolerable compared to the passive aggressive shaming and shunning. Most of the damage was done behind one's back, although the judgements, gossip and lies somehow always found their way back to me, eventually.

It was hard to take it personally, really… for although I may have been the scapegoat in many situations and outcast for not always conforming, watching as an outsider to what it truly took to be accepted into this inner circle was a price I was not willing to pay. Don't get me wrong, I loved these humans and most certainly went out of my way to prove my love to them in every way I knew how. But it was never enough. They would never accept me for living authentically, for the few that controlled how the family operated and kept the dynamic in working order, were living in fear of their own truths. They lied to each other for control, they lied to each other to avoid, and when that was not effective, the result was either an aggressive verbal lashing, the ice-cold shoulder, or both. I was asked to lie. I was asked to apologize for things that everyone involved knew I did not do. And I did it. I covered for others to make their partnerships more comfortable, while mine took the beating. I would take the verbal and emotional beating. I spent years hiding from my own truth, smiling through my pain, until the weight just got too heavy to bear. In trying so desperately to belong, I had never felt so isolated and alone. I had lost myself completely.

I knew I needed to muster up what little strength I had left to search for the woman I once was, but it was my strength that seemed to trigger him. When I would try to talk about something he disagreed with, a need or feeling of mine, it would become a fight. He told me he appreciated that I took care of the way I looked, then called me superficial and shamed me for spending money on skin care products. He told me that I didn't do enough to contribute, even though I had a full-time career, took care of the house that we purchased together, worked part-time as a tutor, and volunteered in our community and church.

Nothing was ever good enough.

One time before a camping trip, I had spent hours packing and getting things ready before he got home to help. I was exhausted but anxious to go on another trip with him, so I walked on eggshells to avoid him as we packed. He always became agitated before trips like that one. So, I pushed through the exhaustion until my body couldn't take any more. I passed out and hit the hardwood floor, and he left me there to continue packing.

His threats in his fits of aggression made my mind and body frozen. One December, I cannot even recall what he was upset about, I just remember his yelling. I had never been so terrified and had my first panic attack. I couldn't breathe or think. It felt as though my whole world was collapsing around me. He stood over me, while I thought I was dying—wishing in the moment that I would—while he continued to berate me for my wrongdoings. In all the chaos of the day, I didn't call to wish my grandma a "happy birthday." She did not survive to celebrate another, and still fills me with regret.

On many occasions he told me that his family, and multiple counselors, thought I was crazy and had a mental health disorder. He demanded that I get help, so I found a counselor and made an appointment. I was happy to attend, hoping it would be helpful. He threatened to track my way there, "just in case."

I have multiple degrees, one of them is a master's in counseling, and I was working as a School Psychologist, but nothing could have prepared me for what was about to transpire. After giving her a summary of my chaotic life, my counselor very empathetically asked me a question.

"Have you ever heard of the cycle of emotional abuse, or seen the visual?"

She pulled out a circular wheel that described the exact pattern of my secret life that I had been living every day, like Groundhog's Day. I had shared this vulnerability with him, and he had preyed on it ... all while making himself the victim. And I had believed him. I cried and he told me how sick he was of me, and insisted that I be put on a timer to limit my time to speak.

I suddenly saw it all for what it was.

And my whole world came crashing down.

How could I have been so naïve? How could I have allowed this to happen? I should have known better. How could anyone take me seriously professionally if I can't choose healthy relationships for myself? How can I even face myself in the mirror, let alone the world? Maybe his family is right? Maybe he is just treating me how I deserve to be treated.

I can't tell you the exact day that it began, as it has been a slow process that continued over time. But what I can tell you is that when I finally hit that breaking point—when I was left so shattered that nothing remained but just fragments of my soul—the healing began. I was finally brought to surrender; and I chose faith. I chose to have faith in God and faith in myself. I chose to trust me. You see, it is in these hardest moments, when we choose to trust ourselves and rely on our faith to guide us through that we find the reprieve we seek. In rebuilding ourselves from scratch, we can be thoughtful and use only the most organic highest quality ingredients. Now looking back on these moments in my life, where true connections were formed in unlikely circumstances, it wasn't unlikely at all. These were moments where I was able to trust myself to be myself *and* be guided by my faith. And it turned out that rebuilding myself wasn't quite as complicated as it had seemed.

I have always been me, but at times with the absence of trust and topped with fear. I am now confidently aware that I am both proud of how I grew up and my humble family values, but also eager to succeed and seek opportunity. I am both an adventure seeker and love nothing more than to be home. I am empathetic and vulnerable and strong, I am humble and intelligent, and now a mother and a warrior. I can be all these things, one at a time or all at once, if that is how I am called.

What matters most is the matter of the heart, and that I trust myself to truly lead from within. I will no longer dull my light to enable someone else's fear of being seen. My hope is that in sharing my journey more souls will be illuminated. As my father would tell me, "Sparkle on, sweetheart," and so I shall.

And so shall you.

⋯ ABOUT MELISA SHELTON

Melisa Shelton is a seasoned school psychologist that has been well received by districts and communities in which she has served. She has received recognition for her achievements and has worked in a variety of settings with a diverse profile of people with varying needs from a plethora of backgrounds. Melisa is passionate about helping children and other adults to meet their full potential both academically, socially, adaptively, and beyond. When not working, Melisa continues to pursue this passion and her faith by volunteering in her community via children's ministry, kid's sports, scouts, mission work, and of course by being a present, active, and loving mother to her own children, Austin and Kinsley. Melisa believes in being a life-long learner and has earned three formal degrees of her own. But what she has come to understand over the many years is that no matter how educated, no matter the culture, the crisis, socioeconomic status, or other such factors, positive progress can be made, and genuine relational trust can be established. It really is all about relationships and learning to trust yourself. Don't be afraid to let your glimmers catch the light and shine.

Facebook: *https://www.facebook.com/melisa.a.shelton*
Instagram: *https://www.instagram.com/melisa_ann949*

12 ⋯ THE ROADMAP HOME TO YOUR AUTHENTIC SELF

by Joanie Elizabeth

Sometimes the journey we are on is not clear. It's blurry or you can feel like you're in a very thick fog. You might feel lost, scared and alone at times. At times sitting in the stillness of night is uncomfortable and lonely. Often, we want to run and hide from our wounds and hurts, and we may feel like we can't reach out to anybody for help because after all, would anyone really understand. Do not be afraid to look up and trust that within you is a light that leads you each step of the way.

I am here to share my journey to give you hope because you *can* take another step forward, you *can* look up from your tears, and you *can* create something better today going forward. If you choose. My journey may look different than yours, but we all have a story to share. No one story is greater or worse than the other; we do not have to hide in the darkness or let fear and shame hold us captive. As Brené Brown says, "When we deny our stories, they define us. When we own our stories, we get to write a brave new ending."

And so, my story begins. It was a spring day, I felt a slight breeze and smelled beautiful roses as I was walking down a pathway holding on to my mama's hand; my older sister holding her other hand. I could smell the beautiful roses along the path and the flowering trees as I looked up. I had felt like I should be happy because we were going to visit a neighbor Mama often had coffee with, while my sister and I played with her five children. But I began to sense something was different with Mama on that breezy spring day. She was trying to smile for us, but something was different. Even as a three-year-old, I could feel it.

When we approached the neighbor's door—as we had done many other days before—Mama quickly gave us a hug and kiss on the cheek. I did not understand what was going on because she wasn't sitting down to have coffee. Instead, she opened the front door, walked back through it, and closed it behind her. I felt so scared, I had never been without her before. What I didn't know, until many years later, was that Mama was having a hard time that day. She had been holding back tears but was trying to be strong for my sister and I, after being forced to go back to work. Her heart had ached deeply when she dropped us off, but she believed our neighbor was a friend, and that my sister and I would be safe and well taken care of while she went to work.

It's still shocking to this day what transpired shortly after Mama walked out that door. I remember crying and tears streaming down my face, I felt so scared. And instead of receiving comfort, Mama's friend had all five of her children and my sister circle around me to chant, "cry baby, cry baby," over and over and over again. I do not remember how long it went on, but it terrified me. I was shaking and crying for my sweet mama, and she was nowhere to be found.

Because I couldn't stop crying, the babysitter took me down to the basement, I believe she locked the door, and left me down there alone. I remember curling up into a tight ball on a big old tan and gold stripped couch, shaking I was so cold and scared. I could hear footsteps walking around above me, and what sounded like water dripping somewhere in the basement. The floor was cold cement, and without windows there was barely any light. I felt terrified. That was the day I lost my voice, sense of self, and the belief that I mattered.

I stayed in the basement until shortly before Mama came to pick me up. We stayed at the babysitter's home for a few more weeks, and during that time I was put in that cold scary basement daily for the slightest tear running down my cheek. I remember the last day, Mama showed up looking very concerned. She took my sister and I to the hospital afterwards. I later found out it was because the babysitter was making my five-year-old sister iron her husband's work clothes, and the iron fell on my sister's arm, leaving a huge painful burn. For many years after she told us how sorry she was.

It only takes one incident to change your view of who you are, dimming your light within you. One moment in life can rob you of many years—even a lifetime—of learning how to re-embrace the light within you. Childhood trauma can especially have a deep impact upon how you view yourself and your value and worth. This deeply traumatic experience caused me to grow up painfully shy; I couldn't look people in the eyes or ask questions. I didn't realize until years later that I had become stuck living out the hurt of my little three-year-old self, who shrunk deep within herself so she would not be hurt or scared again. It became the story I would tell myself over and over again, for many years. I was afraid of confrontation and spent most of my life walking on eggshells. As I was finding my way forward, it became quite the journey. I pushed through many obstacles and carried heavy loads. My pattern of shame and being afraid to speak showed up many times over many years. During those years this pattern continued to show up, as I repeated the cycle of neglect and abuse.

When we experience trauma, we tend to seek out people that are not good for us, without meaning to. I went through some very painful abusive relationships that I had worked hard to navigate through. It took great strength to begin my healing journey. Along the way I saw glimmers of hope in the glimmers of my authentic self, coming back to life. Over time, I learned to look deep within and follow those glimmers. As well, I began to follow nudges that led me to face my fears. This was incredibly uncomfortable, but I did it anyway. I learned what boundaries were and took time to soul search and pay attention to what mattered most to me. I learned to ask myself what I was thinking and feeling, wanting and needing. I was able to unlock the hurt parts of me, specifically that hurt little girl who was afraid to open her mouth and speak. Slowly, I began to heal. I found her and helped her to embrace the beautiful bright light within her through a lot of soul searching, praying, and tracing family history and cycles.

I heard a quote once that deeply resonated with me during this journey, it read, "Happiness isn't something that depends on our surroundings, it's something we make inside ourselves." Eventually, I had to take my full power back to continue evolving and following my dreams, hopes and visions. It was time to say yes—loudly—to share my story in hopes that it will offer a message of hope, healing, light and love to those who need it; to give a blueprint to the way forward for us all to embrace who we are. By embracing the nudge to lead from within, I began to realize that there is nothing wrong with me. Because I was not less than or broken.

When I was blessed to give birth to my first daughter, I wanted to speak up for myself ... for her. After I was blessed with a second daughter, I felt a deep calling to help others learn how to embrace who they are to live an authentic life, free from abuse and abandoning their own wants, needs and desires. This led to my journey of going back to college as a single mom to get an undergraduate degree in psychology. While I was still raising my daughters, I followed another nudge to continue my education for a master's degree.

Throughout my education, there were many times I had to speak in front of a classroom. I felt sick to my stomach, turned bright red, and would shake. I began to question myself, asking what do *I* have to offer others? Through this inner questioning, I began to realize that I was still afraid to speak. I was still operating out of survival mode from my trauma. Once I embraced the nudge that was leading me deep within myself, I began to grow into a whole self, not just the pieces that still felt damaged.

One day it all came together. I stopped abandoning myself and started to pay attention to what I needed and wanted. I began to speak up for myself and learn what boundaries were, how to apply them, and not feel guilty for saying "yes" to my own needs. I stood up for my hurt sad and scared three-year-old self and let go of all the broken pieces. I chose to stand up for myself, my daughters, granddaughters, sisters and other women. I realized that I had been helping women all along. I owned and embraced how I am changing the world, simply by shining my light brighter for whoever may need to see it.

Often, we don't realize that we are operating from of a trauma lens, living our lives as less than who we were designed to be. And so, we settle for bare the minimum; crumbs that are less than what we deserve. We lose track of the dreams we had as a child and what we are most passionate about. Because when we've been through trauma, it changes pathways in our brains. The good news is that we can rewire our anxious brains to heal the roots of our trauma. And we can step into who we were meant to be.

Once we learn to follow the inner light that burns within us, we can heal and grow into the woman we were are designed to be. We learn to thrive in our lives, not just survive. We have the power to create a new healing blueprint for our lives by owning our own path. We learn that it is safe to come out and walk in the light, and not hide in the darkness or shame that doesn't belong to us.

If you've ever experienced childhood trauma, or even adulthood trauma, you may have become a people pleaser. I call this a human *doing* instead of a human *being*. A human *doing* is someone who becomes a shell of themselves. Someone who believes they are valued by the things they do. And so, they will do what they can to make sure everyone else is happy and their needs are met, even if it means they must absorb the energy of someone else and walk on eggshells to keep the peace. But a human *being* believes their self-worth is defined by their values, attitudes and beliefs. By who they are. A human *being* is someone who leads from their light deep within. She knows how she feels, has a clear sense of self, can notice what she needs, isn't afraid to ask for help when she needs it, and sets clear boundaries with herself and others. She values herself *and* her needs.

We must learn to not abandon ourselves, learn to recognize what we need from the inside out and remember our needs are just as important as anybody else's. Often, we get lost—the false identity of who we've become—like something on a clearance rack. And while we all may like a good sale, our value and self-worth do *not* belong on a clearance rack. Yes, there's been times over the years that my hurt little three-year-old self tried to show up, telling me I can't open my mouth and speak because I'm too shy. But I'm happy to say that today my three-year-old self shines brightly. I no longer operate out of survival mode, I have found my authentic self.

Today, I now own and operate my own private practice and have helped thousands of people find the key to unlock their own trauma and embrace their light to find their way forward. In their healing journeys, they also have broken free from darkness and the prison they held themselves captives in to welcome their authentic selves home—free to be who they are designed to be. I also inspire and encourage others by doing vlogs on social media. And as I'm writing in this chapter, I'm preparing to add another platform to my journey of supporting others by launching a podcast titled, *Adventure to Wellness: Your Roadmap Home to Your Authentic Self.*

You are a rare treasure. Always remember that. Remember that your needs are just as important as everyone else's. You are emerging and transforming into the most amazing person you can possibly become. Don't let other people define you, don't hold yourself captive by the comparison game, or what others say about you. You are a one-of-a-kind masterpiece, and you can create and design whatever you believe you can. It may require that you first shed layers of hurt and wounds—as well as low self-esteem—before you are able to embrace growing into the beautiful person you were meant to be. The love that you give to everyone else, you deserve to give it to yourself too.

You also deserve your own time and attention. You deserve to check in with yourself and notice that your needs matter just as much as anyone else's. When you decide to make yourself a priority and not abandon yourself, you will no longer settle for crumbs or less than you deserve.

It's never too late to step forward and create something amazing for your life if you choose to. Remember people will love at their own level of self-love, they will communicate to their own level of self-awareness, and they will behave to their own level of healed trauma. Release the past, embrace today to stay in the moment, and embrace all that your heart desires to create for your life.

···ABOUT JOANIE ELIZABETH

Joanie Elizabeth's determination to empower her daughters and protect them from the effects of divorce grew into a spirit of resilience that has been a cornerstone of her life, reflecting her passion for helping others. She pursued this passion academically, earning a bachelor's degree in Psychology, followed by a master's degree in Applied Behavioral Science. Her professional journey is driven by a profound desire to assist individuals in navigating life's challenges, recognizing the impact of familial influences on our psyche. Joanie believes that our early familial environments shape our perceptions of "normal," often limiting our potential. With eighteen years of experience in the mental health field, Joanie's approach is centered on uncovering the inherent strength and insights within her clients, guiding them to find meaning and value in their struggles. Her ability to identify and nurture the unique qualities of those she works with has defined her successful career in private practice. Beyond her professional life, Joanie cherishes time spent with her daughter and grandchildren, finding joy in outdoor activities and beach outings.

Joanie is the founder of Northwest Counseling, where she combines her roles as a therapist, writer and speaker to inspire and uplift others. Her content, whether through vlogging or speaking engagements, draws on her personal experiences and professional insights to offer encouragement and support. Additionally, Joanie is launching an innovative podcast with her daughter, titled, *Adventure to Wellness: Your Roadmap Home to Your Authentic Self,* which will feature discussions on mental health and nutrition from the perspectives of a Licensed Mental Health Counselor and a Licensed Registered Dietitian Nutritionist.

13 ··· HEALING ENERGY

by Donita Wheeler

"Donita, this time it's melanoma."

Those were the words that hit me like a ton of bricks, marking the fifth time I received the devastating news that cancer had invaded my body. Each instance of this relentless disease had presented its own unique challenges and hardships, taking me through a seemingly never-ending rollercoaster of emotions. Little did I know that amidst the chaos and despair, cancer had brought me an unexpected gift—one that would allow me to rediscover a dormant talent.

As I reflect on my journey, I now understand that the Universe has a way of persistently delivering the lessons we need until we truly comprehend their significance. I was shocked when I found out that I had been diagnosed with cancer for the fifth time, and to make matters worse, this particular type of cancer required a significant alteration to my physical appearance.

It was a mere four weeks before my son's wedding when I underwent a surgical procedure that involved removing the upper portion of my ear and utilizing the skin from the back of my neck to reconstruct it. I distinctly remember the moment when the surgeon asked me about my hairstyle preference for my son's wedding.

"Well, I guess that depends on you, doc!" I responded in a lighthearted manner.

Ultimately, I made the decision to wear my hair in an updo, as my ear had fully healed by then. It was during this time that I truly embraced and rediscovered my genuine, authentic self. The experience of facing yet another cancer diagnosis and undergoing a procedure that altered my appearance was undoubtedly challenging. However, it also served as a catalyst for personal growth and self-acceptance. As I stood before the mirror, observing my reconstructed ear and contemplating my hairstyle for the wedding, I realized that my physical appearance did not define me. Instead, it was my inner strength, resilience and ability to adapt that truly mattered.

Choosing to wear my hair in an updo was a symbolic gesture of embracing my transformed self. It was a way of confidently showcasing my reconstructed ear and celebrating the journey I had been through. In that moment, I felt a renewed sense of empowerment and authenticity. It was a significant milestone for me. It was a public declaration of my triumph over adversity and a testament to my unwavering spirit. As I watched my son exchange vows with his love, I couldn't help but feel an overwhelming sense of gratitude for the strength and resilience that had carried me through my cancer journey.

This experience taught me the importance of embracing and accepting ourselves, regardless of any physical changes or challenges we may face. It reminded me that true beauty lies in our ability to embrace our authentic selves and find strength in our vulnerabilities. Through this journey, I not only rediscovered my genuine self but also learned to appreciate the beauty and strength that can arise from adversity. For the first time, I understood that denial and fear had previously kept me from truly understanding the profound lessons that cancer had to offer.

The most significant lesson I learned was the rediscovery of my innate ability to read energy. This gift had always been a part of me, but I had buried it deep within, longing to be seen as "normal" by societal standards. I had dismissed my intuition and ignored the subtle energetic vibrations that permeated every interaction and experience. As a child, I had the unique ability to see beyond the surface and understand what was truly happening energetically. It wasn't a visual or sensory experience, but rather a deep understanding of the energetic emotions and thoughts of others. I could look at someone and read their energetic state, whether it be joy, sadness or something else entirely. This skill extended beyond individuals and could even be applied to situations or environments.

For example, I remember wondering why my friend Ted's house wasn't selling. In my mind, I would focus on Ted's house and instantly see its energy. It was clear to me that the house was filled with a heavy, sad energy. I knew that no one would want to buy a house with such a negative energy, even if they couldn't consciously explain why it made them feel that way. I then used my ability to shift the energy of the house, infusing it with balanced, joyful love, gratitude, and a touch of authenticity. And just like that, the house sold within days.

I had always possessed this unique skill, but let's be honest, it was considered weird by societal standards, especially in the eighties. I didn't want to be labeled as the "weirdo," so I suppressed this part of myself for a long time. However, my journey with cancer forced me to confront and embrace my true self, including this ability to read energy. It became clear to me that this gift was not something to be ashamed of, but rather a powerful tool for healing and understanding. Cancer taught me the importance of authenticity and embracing our unique gifts, no matter how unconventional they may seem. I have learned to trust my intuition and honor the energetic vibrations that guide me. I have come to appreciate the beauty and power of energy and its impact on our lives.

Cancer may have been a challenging and painful experience, but it also served as a catalyst for self-discovery and acceptance. Now, I proudly embrace my ability to read energy and use it to bring healing and positivity into the world. I no longer fear being seen as "weird," because I understand that my authenticity is what makes me truly special. Cancer taught me to embrace my true self, and for that, I am forever grateful. It was cancer that served as the catalyst for the reawakening of this extraordinary ability, shaking me out of the illusion of normalcy and inviting me to embrace my true self. And through this incredibly challenging journey, I have come to realize that cancer is not just a physical battle; it is a spiritual and emotional odyssey as well.

Each time I faced the diagnosis, I was compelled to confront my deepest fears, question the meaning of life, and reevaluate my priorities. It was during these moments of vulnerability that my intuitive senses sharpened, allowing me to tap into the energetic frequencies that surround us all. The lessons cancer has taught me extend far beyond the physical realm. They have encouraged me to embrace my authenticity, to honor the whispers of my intuition, and to live in alignment with my true purpose. Through this gift of heightened perception, I have learned to navigate life's challenges with a newfound sense of clarity and understanding.

In sharing my story, I hope to inspire others who may be facing their own battles with cancer or other adversities. Live in your authenticity. Know that within the darkest moments lie hidden gifts, waiting to be discovered. Embrace the lessons being offered to you, even if they arrive in the form of unwelcome experiences. We are all capable of accessing our inner wisdom and reconnecting with our unique gifts—whether it be the ability to read energy, to create art, to inspire others through words or actions, run a multimillion dollar company, or to simply offer compassion and love.

It took me quite some time to fully grasp the connection between my ability to read energy and truly understanding what I was reading. It was a gradual process that unfolded over the course of about ten years. Looking back, I can now see how each struggle and challenge I faced was necessary for my own personal growth and transformation. It's not something I can share, as it's as unique to me as my fingerprint. At first, it was hard to comprehend why I had to endure such a relentless series of battles. Why couldn't one battle be enough to teach me the lessons I needed? But I came to realize that each experience was uniquely tailored to my own personal path and the lessons I needed to learn.

Life has a way of presenting us with the exact circumstances and challenges that will push us to grow and evolve. It's not always easy to understand or accept in the moment, but looking back, I can see how each struggle was an opportunity for me to learn, heal, and become more aligned with my true self. Through my journey with cancer and the subsequent exploration of my ability to read energy, I have come to understand that our personal paths are filled with lessons that are meant specifically for us. What may seem like a series of unrelated challenges is actually a carefully orchestrated sequence of events designed to help us grow, learn and become the best version of ourselves.

It's important to remember that everyone's path is unique, and what may be a lesson for one person may not be the same for another. We each have our own set of experiences and challenges that are meant to guide us on our individual journeys. So, while it may be tempting to compare our struggles to those of others or question why we must face certain obstacles, it's important to trust in the process and have faith that everything is happening for a reason.

Each challenge we encounter is an opportunity for growth and transformation, and it is through these experiences that we can truly understand ourselves and our purpose in life. In the end, it's all about embracing our own personal path and the lessons that come with it. By doing so, we can navigate through life with a greater sense of purpose, understanding and authenticity.

The lessons cancer brought to me forced me to confront my own beliefs, attitudes and habits, and to reassess my priorities and the way I lived my life. The experience taught me the value of resilience, inner strength, and the necessity of cherishing each precious moment. I was able to use my ability to read energy in a new way, I was able to see patterns.

As I navigated the ups and downs of my illness, I began to understand that our thoughts, emotions and actions all carry energy that shapes the world around us. I learned that negative thoughts and emotions can create destructive patterns, keeping us stuck in cycles of despair, hopelessness and illness. Conversely, by cultivating positive energy through gratitude, self-compassion and self-care, I witnessed how it can shift our patterns towards healing, growth and success. I realized that I had the power to break free from limiting beliefs and patterns that no longer served me.

The more I learned about patterns, the more I embraced the exploration of these patterns, I realized that they were not merely random occurrences, but profound lessons in disguise. Each moment of triumph carried the message of resilience, reminding me of the strength within me that could weather any storm. Every setback whispered the importance of patience, teaching me to persevere with unwavering determination. The cycle of hope and despair showcased the delicate dance between vulnerability and courage, urging me to embody both with grace.

As I began to unravel the hidden layers of my being. I discovered an unyielding spirit, a reservoir of hope and love that refused to be extinguished. I was onto something. Using my momentum, I began to dig into the world of energy healing and alternative therapies. I devoured books, attended workshops, and sought out practitioners who could offer insights into the unseen forces at play.

Being able to read energy is one thing, but truly understanding it is a whole different level. I had mastered the skill of reading energy, but now it was time to delve deeper and decipher its meaning. And beyond that, I wanted to learn how to utilize this ability to serve others and help them become the best version of themselves.

I learned that our bodies are not just physical entities but are also composed of subtle energy fields, intricately connected to our emotions, thoughts and experiences. These energy fields, often referred to as chakras, act as gateways through which life force energy flows. When these energy centers become imbalanced or blocked, it can manifest as physical or emotional ailments. I then began to observe the patterns within my own energy field. I noticed how certain emotions, such as fear or anger, seemed to be lodged in specific areas of my body. These stagnant energies created blockages, hindering the flow of vital life force energy, and contributing to the progression of my illness.

Inspired by this revelation, I embarked on a mission to cleanse and rebalance my energy field. I sought out various modalities, from Reiki to sound healing, to help release the trapped energies and restore harmony within. Each session brought a sense of relief and renewal, as if I was shedding layers of energetic baggage that no longer served me. The patterns were still there, lingering around, I knew that there was more.

It wasn't just about the physical practices; it was also about the inner work. I continued into the depths of my psyche, exploring the emotional wounds and limiting beliefs that had contributed to the manifestation of cancer in my life.

Through therapy, meditation and journaling, I confronted my fears, forgave myself and others, and cultivated a deep sense of self-love and acceptance. I began clearing my energy and as I was clearing the energy, I could see it was attached to a particular time in my life—a particular age. Then as I stepped outside myself, I could see that this energy was the catalyst to the patterns that were literally trying to kill me. This was pivotal moment.

I then noticed a shift within myself. The cycles of hope and despair became less intense, replaced by a steady sense of resilience and inner peace. I no longer saw cancer as an enemy to be defeated but as a teacher, guiding me towards a deeper understanding of myself and the world around me. The cancer allowed me to see the energies, to read the energies, and to understand how the energies acted with clearing and high vibrations. With each passing day, I became more attuned to the subtle energies that permeated my being. I could sense the ebb and flow of life force energy, the vibrations of the universe resonating within me. It was as if I had tapped into a wellspring of wisdom and intuition, guiding me towards choices and actions that aligned with my highest good. I began to break the patterns formed in my body from my past experiences using all the new things had learned.

The process of unraveling the mysteries of my ability to read energy was a journey that I can't fully explain. It felt as if I was pulling on a thread of yarn on my sweater, and with each tug, new insights and understanding unfolded before me. It was as if messages were being transmitted to me, not from my own mind, but from a higher source. These messages continued to flow through me, bringing me knowledge and understanding that I couldn't have obtained through conventional means. It was a profound experience that allowed me to see things with a newfound clarity.

One day, during this journey, I had a revelation that each of my cells contained a unique, multi-colored stacking in chronological order. This stacking was present in every single cell of my being. It was a remarkable realization that each cell held a visual representation of my life's experiences, neatly arranged in a chronological sequence. The colors and patterns within each cell told a story, capturing the essence of my journey and the lessons I had learned along the way.

This insight opened my eyes to the interconnectedness of my physical and energetic being. It showed me that every aspect of my being, down to the cellular level, held a record of my experiences and growth. Understanding this intricate stacking within my cells allowed me to appreciate the depth and complexity of my own existence. It reminded me that every experience, every challenge, and every triumph had contributed to shaping the person I had become.

This newfound understanding also sparked a desire within me to utilize my ability to read energy to help others. I realized that if I could see and understand the unique stacking within my own cells, perhaps I could assist others in uncovering the hidden layers within themselves. I successfully eliminated all the stacked energy in my cells, freeing myself from holding onto any energy that was causing my patterns to persist. Interestingly, some patterns served as motivators, while others seemed to remain untouched.

Feeling liberated and light, I immediately started on a program for clients to remove their stacked energy and move forward in life with patterns that serve them. It was at that moment—the moment I finished writing my program out and preparing to market for clients—that I had two clients land in my lap, and I have gone on to help hundreds. The healer within me was now offering services to those seeking solace and transformation, one person at a time, raising their vibration and the earth's vibration. It is a successful program, through workshops, one-on-one sessions, and online resources, I guide individuals on their own journeys of stacked energy removal, energy cleansing and self-discovery.

Each person I encounter has their own unique patterns and challenges to overcome. Some carry the weight of past traumas, while others struggle with limiting beliefs and self-doubt. I am able to read each individual and guide them through their own energy program. Together, we unravel the patterns that are holding them back, creating space for healing, growth and empowerment. Rewriting the patterns and replacing the old energy with new charged energy making them a magnet for manifestations. Through this process of rewriting patterns and infusing new energy, individuals experience profound shifts in their lives. They shed the limitations that once defined them and embrace a newfound sense of freedom and possibility. As they release the stacked energy, they make room for abundance, joy, and fulfillment to flow effortlessly into their lives.

It was not a quick fix or a temporary solution. It required commitment, self-reflection, and a willingness to confront and release deep-seated patterns. With each step forward, individuals experienced a profound sense of liberation and empowerment. They discover that they have the power to shape their own reality and create a life that aligns with their deepest desires.

In my ever-expanding journey of assisting others in their transformation, I recognize that there are specific areas of life where many individuals desire additional guidance and support beyond the Stacked Energy Removal Program. Money and relationships, being two fundamental aspects of our lives, are prime candidates for specialized programs.

The money program I developed dives into the energetic patterns and beliefs surrounding abundance and prosperity. By helping individuals identify and release any limiting beliefs or blockages they may have around money, I empower them to align with the flow of abundance that exists in the universe. Through various energy clearing techniques and practical exercises, I guide them in creating a positive and abundant mindset, attracting financial opportunities, and managing their resources in a way that aligns with their highest good. The success stories that emerge from this program have been truly remarkable, as individuals experience a significant shift in their financial circumstances and a newfound sense of abundance and security.

Similarly, the relationship program focuses on the energetic dynamics that underlie our connections with others, whether they be romantic partnerships, friendships or family relationships. Through an in-depth exploration of energetic patterns, communication styles and self-love practices, I help individuals unravel any unhealthy dynamics and foster healthier and more fulfilling relationships. This program brings healing, growth, and increased harmony to many, enabling them to cultivate deeper connections and experience more love and joy in their interactions.

These programs have proven to be immensely valuable for those seeking transformation and growth in these specific areas of their lives. By combining energy healing techniques with practical tools and personalized guidance, I aim to support individuals in creating lasting, positive change and achieving their desired outcomes.

It has been a tumultuous path, filled with pain and uncertainty, but it has also been a journey of self-discovery, resilience and unwavering gratitude. Cancer has challenged me to redefine my limits, to break free from the constraints of societal norms, and to embrace the true essence of who I am. It has given me the strength to rise above adversity and to find profound beauty in the midst of chaos. I am forever changed, forever grateful, and forever ready to embrace whatever lies ahead. Cancer may have taken a part of me, but it has also given me so much more in return.

It fills my heart with joy to witness the profound transformations that take place within those who commit themselves to these programs. Seeing individuals reclaim their power, embrace their worthiness, and manifest their desires is a testament to the incredible potential that lies within each and every one of us. I am deeply grateful for the opportunity to serve and guide others on their unique journeys of healing, growth and self-discovery.

···ABOUT DONITA WHEELER

Donita Wheeler, the visionary founder of Donita Mamabear LLC, is a beacon of hope and inspiration. She triumphed over cancer not once, but five times, a testament to her unwavering resilience. Donita is not just a survivor; she's a best-selling author renowned for works like *BareMyself*, *The Lemonade Stand*, and *A-Z Spirituality*. As an esteemed energetic therapist, she empowers clients by helping them break free from restrictive energetic patterns, drawing from her personal experiences and profound expertise. Under her insightful guidance, individuals embark on transformative journeys marked by profound healing and enduring fulfillment. Donita's exceptional narrative and her role through Donita Mamabear LLC highlight the boundless potential of the human spirit. Her work exemplifies the transformative power of dedicated guidance in facilitating personal growth and healing. Donita is resolutely committed to helping others unlock their potential, leading them to lives enriched by vitality, purpose and profound well-being.

Website: *https://www.donitamamabear.com*
Facebook: *https://www.facebook.com/DonitaMamaBear*
Instagram: *https://www.instagram.com/donitamamabear*

14 ··· WALKING: FINDING INTUITIVE THOUGHT, STEP BY STEP

by Deanna Nowadnick

Sometimes the smallest step in the right direction ends up being the biggest step of your life. Tiptoe is you must, but take the step. -Naeem Callaway

I stepped on the scale, braced for the worst. I looked down at the digital display flashing the verdict: eight pounds! *Eight pounds?* I grimaced and stepped back. Looking in the mirror, I ripped into my reflection.

Really, eight pounds? You're away on vacation eight days and you're up eight pounds? How does that happen?

But I knew exactly how it happened, how it's happened for years. I've had a love-hate relationship with food since I was a teen. At a formative time, I learned to cope with stress, disappointment, and even excitement by stuffing myself with food. Beginning in high school, my type-A determination, troublesome strength, and misdirected resolve all found solace in a binge-purge cycle that consumed my afternoons. Not sure how to deal with new and unfamiliar emotions, I pushed them down and away with soda crackers dipped in raspberry jam. I used saltines and simple sugars to nurture and sustain me, comfort and soothe, celebrate and grieve, and before the end of my sophomore year, I was in the throes of an eating disorder. I knew intuitively that food wasn't the answer, but I didn't know what else to do. And rather than grasp at straws, I grabbed at food. What started as a teenaged stumble on the road to emotional maturity became a decades-long coping mechanism for the vagaries of life.

I'm no longer that lost and confused teenager, but I still struggle with days that don't go well, challenging afternoons, and times of sadness. My insecurities and sense of unworthiness too often define me, and food can soften the blow. Simple sugars can take away the sting. I've also learned to turn to food on days that do go well, at times of special accomplishment, also moments of great joy. Those same simple sugars and savory carbs can provide a quiet moment of pleasure and celebration.

But then, I get back from an eight-day vacation—a wonderful time away with family—step on the scale, and all those feelings of frustration and disgust, shame and contempt, come flooding back.

Miserable Steps

Looking back, I recall memories of that family vacation; one that *had* been absolutely wonderful. My husband Kurt and I met our two boys and their families at our favorite resort on the bend of the Columbia River in Eastern Washington. We delighted in our time with grandsons, Enzo and Austin, both three years old. We took boat rides and splashed in the pool. We took stroller rides and played in the sand. And I'd eaten my way through it all. Through the giggles and our moments at the playground. I overate at breakfast, lunch and dinner. I snacked all day long. And eight days and eight pounds later, I looked down at the scale in disgust, trying hard to remember the wonderful times while I stared at my pronounced flaws. I stepped away and stood in front of the mirror. My body shuddered; my shoulders slumped. I was so tired of being emotionally tethered to food. Feeling bad, I eat. Feeling good, I eat. Feeling anything, I eat. I had to get away from the scale and the mirror. But not knowing what else to do, I decided to take a walk.

My spirits low, my heart heavy, I stepped outside and began a miserable twenty-minute slog around the block. Yes, a miserable slog. On a beautiful summer morning, my feet balked with every step. The fresh air stung my cheeks. I barely looked ahead, afraid that every passing car, every neighbor would surely recognize my shame. That morning I could not have imagined my time outside would be the first of 1193 (and counting!) consecutive walks. That such an accomplishment could come from such disappointment and frustration overwhelms me—in the best way.

Quiet, Peaceful Steps

So often we expect our accomplishments to come from those moments we plan for, from the care and attention given to the steps we take, the direction we go, the decisions we make, that small inner voice that says, "Go get 'em!"

Yes, we'll have setbacks and challenges, situations in which we rally our "I can do this!" fortitude, but rarely do we expect to find accomplishments in misery and defeat, shame and struggle. I didn't. But a second walk followed the first and my spirits became not quite as low—

my heart not quite as heavy. My feet balked a little less; the air stung a bit less. I waved at a car I recognized, smiled at a neighbor. The sun warming my intentions, I decided to walk every day for eight days. Perhaps I'd be able to walk off the eight pounds!

I did not walk off the eight pounds, but I did walk off a couple, so I decided after eight days that I'd walk eight more. I walked around the block. I walked around a small lake in town. I walked to the post office and my favorite coffee shop. Each day I found thirty to forty minutes to be outside in the fresh air.

After sixteen days of walking, I stepped into September, that special time each year when we find ourselves ready for the new and the next. This time I turned the page of my calendar and decided to start the new school year walking the next thirty days. I added a tickler on my computer, a box I could check off each day. I downloaded a weather app on my phone, so I could plan. By the end of September, my walks had given me a new rhythm to the day. I watched summer become fall. I felt the air cool. I saw the leaves turn from green to red and orange, yellow and brown before falling about my feet. I listened to the soft tap of raindrops on my umbrella, birds calling, and a distant train announcing its arrival into town. With my walks came a lightness in my being, not a weight loss— although I did lose another couple pounds—but a newfound peacefulness. Disconnected from the scale, away from my computer, television, and phone, I found an unexpected quiet. And in the quiet, I found time to sort through the emotions of the day: the phone call that didn't go well, the anticipated busyness of the morning, the joy of a FaceTime chat with my grandson. I could just "be" with my emotions.

I still cringe, remembering the tone in my voice while speaking with a customer service representative who wasn't providing customer service. I planned for that busy day, creating order to the many tasks ahead. I smiled, thinking about my next call with Austin. Rather than push my emotions down and away, I walked with them, both the good ones and the not-so-good ones. I fussed over some situations walk after walk after walk and then one day I didn't. While finishing up edits on my third book, I would get upset with changes that needed to be made. Chapters that I thought insightful and interesting came back from my editor with questions, revisions and lots of red ink. After several days of moping, I would near the end of my walk and think, *Oh, goodness! She's right!*

While walking I had a chance to deal with old feelings, some stirred up by new experiences. When Kurt's mom died, I walked with her memory for miles. I also used the time to reflect on the passing of my own mother. I thought about other changes in me and surrounding me. A friend was moving away. My joints ached in ways they hadn't before. At times my heart hurt.

Brisk Steps with God

Most important, I began to hear a voice within: God's voice. I'm a woman of faith. I'd like to believe I'm a woman of *great* faith; someone who walks with God each and every day. But honestly, my relationship with God can get very one-sided, my prayers a laundry list of wants for me and to-dos for God. I delight in looking back and seeing God in the details of my life, but I'm not so good at waiting on him for guidance and direction in the moment.

More than once, he's found me walking at a rather brisk pace, looking over my shoulder and asking that he keep up. Until things don't go well. Then I'm beseeching God's help, hands tightly folded, eyes tightly closed. Resounding through my prayer is a "Please, God! Please, God!" litany, but still working through life at that rather brisk pace, I rarely wait around for his answer, not sure how we're supposed to "hear" God or "see" his direction. Until I started walking. Until I got away from my desk and the phone, my to-do list and my wish list.

Not long after I took my first walk, I started going live each week inside the Fave Lifestyles Women's Group on Facebook. My "Morning WOLK with God" was a ten-minute segment in which I shared "words of loving kindness" with the ladies of Fave. Each week. Every Friday I needed to have something to say. My priority was to share something from God. I wanted my message to be his message, but I was stumped.

How do I do that?

My walks became a time to plan for Friday "WOLKs." But not at first. Early on I used those first miles to fuss and fume: *Why am I doing this? Dear God, was there no one else? Absolutely no one? What do I talk about? Every. Single. Week!* And then in the stillness of my steps, an idea would come. One week I talked about an errand that became more than an errand when I picked a friend up at the train station. Another Friday I marveled at a lesson in grace I got after leaving my phone on the roof of my car. Yes, while driving! Each week messages would come, all connecting to God's love and faithfulness and bigger, more important lessons in life.

When I said yes to "Morning WOLKs with God," I began making a list of possible topics, but it went unused. My ideas were always replaced by inspirational ideas that came to me during my walks. Whenever I tried to "bank" a couple ideas, they never worked. But messages from walking always worked. They were timely, insightful and inspirational. And there it was: God's guidance from within.

Insightful, Inspirational Steps

Knowing God was leading me and directing me in my WOLKs each week, I began to see him leading and directing me in other moments, through other situations, during the planned and unplanned, the expected and unexpected. I found myself listening for him, watching for him, waiting for that feeling from within. Some of his guidance came in the wisdom of family and friends; some of his direction came in the advice and counsel of colleagues and those around me. But I didn't recognize and appreciate his guidance and direction until I got away from my desk, away from my television and computer and away from my phone during my daily walks. Looking back, I smile at the woman whose frustration and disappointment found her fleeing the scale and stumbling out the door for that miserable slog around the block. What started as an escape from a seemingly impossible situation became an opportunity to take my faith to a deeper, more personal level. My walks were also a chance to develop some emotional muscle. And it happened on the more difficult days.

Steps in the Rain

As you would imagine, some walks were absolutely beautiful; some were not. A couple days were so stormy, my umbrella blew inside out. Other days were hot and I sweated. Some days were so cold I wore tights and an extra sweater underneath my coat with handwarmers inside my gloves, muffs on my ears. There were days the rain left me drenched, even using an umbrella. Several days I had to tell myself, "It's just forty minutes," and then repeat it again and again throughout my walk. Oh, how often I needed to remind myself saying, "it's just forty minutes." Whether walking or making my way through the day.

For all of us, there are times when we think, *I can't do this. I don't want to do this.* A difficult work assignment looms large. A challenging call needs to be made. And then there's that meeting you'd really like to postpone. Better yet, cancel. But rain-soaked moments can motivate us in ways not expected. No one wants to wade through the difficult, the uncomfortable, the torrential downpours in life. I'd rather my day unfolded calmly, predictably, latte at my side. A popular sports brand wants us to "just do it," but some days I just don't want to. I want to avoid it, cancel it, pretend it's not there. Walking in the rain and the wind—and when it's a little warmer than I'd like—has given me an extra measure of emotional fortitude when life takes a turn. Sometimes it's navigating bumps in the road, sometimes it's when all I want to do is eat something, anything, everything, and flush away the anxiety, uncertainty, and irritations.

When I was a child, my mom would ask that I count to ten when upset. Perhaps your mom did too. My walks have become an adult version of her encouragement. My walks help me to push the "pause" button on the day. My walks give me time to clear my head, organize my thoughts, and on occasion, calm down. I have time to be sad and angry, happy and content. I can just be with my feelings, rather than grab a simple carb. Now I grab a little time. Outside. In the fresh air. Some days I'll walk early, giving me some time to prepare for what's to come. Some days I'll walk mid-day or later in the day, giving me time to process what's been.

The Right Steps

And when I pause, I have found that I'm better able to take steps in the right direction, especially when trying to deal with the harder parts to the day, also the most exciting. Because some days stuff happens, both good and bad. And during my walks, I have time to reflect. Because it's often while I'm talking to the birds and admiring the neighbor's hedge roses that the answers come—from within, from God. I turn the corner, take a deep breath, and think *Oh, God! That's it!*

Self-care. I was never quite sure what that meant, what that looked like, how to make that a part of my life. Gym memberships came and went along with monthly massages and coffee dates with the girls. And then frustration and failure pushed me out the door. Walking outside has helped me heal inside. Walking every day has given me time with my feelings— every day. But most important, walking has helped me find God—in the details, in the moment, in the opportunities—every day.

I don't know how I'm going to manage the next 1193 walks. Had you told me that first miserable day that I was starting an adventure that would stretch into years, I'd have said, *No way!* I would have stopped before starting, not believing I could do it. The idea was too big. The idea of connecting with my feelings was too overwhelming. Even today I can think of nothing I've done for 1193 days, except eat and sleep, shower and dab on mascara. But I don't have to plan for the next 1193 walks. I can grab a little mascara and just plan for today.

The Next Steps

Some thoughts if you'd like to add a walk to your day:

Plan one walk, today's walk.

- You don't need to plan 1193 walks. You're looking at your calendar for the best time today.
- I was careful not to say, "I'm going to walk every day before breakfast." That plan will work some days, but not others. Instead let each day unfold as it's going to unfold, grabbing time when it works best.
- Use the weather app on your phone. I love catching a break between rain showers. I don't walk after it get too warm.

Disconnect.

- Leave the earbuds at your desk. Mute your phone. Delight in the sounds of your neighborhood. Listen for the voice within.
- Walk as far as you walk.
- I was also careful not to say, "I'm going to walk three miles every day." Instead, I found longer and shorter routes that worked for longer and shorter time slots.

Change it up.

- Some days I walked around the block. Other days I walked to the post office. One Saturday I walked a 5k with my husband. One spring we walked around Disneyland with the grandchildren.

Enjoy the company of others.

- I thoroughly enjoyed my time alone outside, but I also treasured the walks I got to take with my husband, Kurt. Some days we walked in a loving stillness. At other times, we regaled each other with story after story. Kurt also helped me on several occasions when I was physically and emotionally without the energy to take the smallest step. Together we made it happen. Think about that special person who can make it happen with you.

Delight in the possibilities.

- Walking gives you time with you. Delight in it. Honor it. Cherish it.
- Finding time to reconnect with yourself is the gift of opportunity.

Steps of Lasting Significance

Yes, a gift of opportunity. Every day—for 1193 days—I've had a chance to connect with me. I've felt the joy of accomplishment and the ache of missteps. I've laughed and groaned. I've marveled at the blue heron who greets me with a flyover, also the family of coots. Each day, each walk, each step has had its own uniqueness. Every day a few minutes outside has helped me better appreciate what I'm feeling inside, inside of me, inside my emotions, inside my head and my heart. Because every day, every task, every conversation has its own uniqueness. And when I'm better in touch with me, I'm better able to respond intuitively, to lead from within.

Is walking the answer to all our problems? No, but it might help with some. Is walking a miracle cure for what ails us? No, but it might help with others. Is walking the answer to prayer? Actually, on some days, it is. Your gift of opportunity, too.

··· ABOUT DEANNA NOWADNICK

Deanna Nowadnick is a writer and speaker who loves helping women of faith connect our delightfully ordinary stories to God's extraordinary love and faithfulness, so we can be encouraged and empowered knowing God's been in the details—always has been, always will be.

Deanna is the author of two books, Fruit of My Spirit and Signs in Life. Coming soon is Bouquet of Wisdom, reflections celebrating not only God's love but also his care. Yes, lots of stories.

When not writing, Deanna manages an investment advisory firm on Mercer Island. She's active in her church, enjoying Bible study and also serving on the leadership team. Her leisure time is filled with knitting and needlepoint, bike rides in the sunshine, and vanilla ice cream bars with a high calorie count.

Deanna lives in Monroe with her husband, Kurt. She is the mother of two adult sons and the mother-in-law of two delightful young ladies. She is also the grandmother to Enzo Antonio, Austin William, and Cameron Spencer. Playdates are the best!

Get *Bouquet of Wisdom* here: *https://a.co/d/ibDrqE1*
Meet Deanna Nowadnick here: *https://deannanowadnick.com*

15 ··· SHIFT HAPPENS

by Briggette Rockett

Her silence roars loud but her meekness is seen as a weakness. For those around not knowing, "meekness is an attitude or quality of heart whereby a person is willing to accept and submit without resistance to the will and desire of someone else." In the case of Christians, this meekness is shown before God. Meekness is mildness, a gentleness of spirit or humility. Meekness models the humility of Jesus Christ. In the Bible meekness means, "a calm temper of mind, not easily provoked." (James 3:13) "Peculiar promises are made to the meek." (Matthew 5:5; Isaiah 66:2) "The meek will inherit the land and enjoy peace and prosperity." (Psalm 37:11)

My meekness had those around me believing they could take advantage of me; my gentle spirit was seen as nothing more than feebleness for them to use and abuse. Have you ever felt taken advantage of because you were seen as easy prey, a punching bag for those who felt empowered to control you?

I was voiceless. I didn't know how to roar; my power within was untapped, unseen with no awareness of its existence. I was hiding behind a mask of insecurities, only believing my looks were all I had to offer. But the funny thing is that I never thought I was pretty, I just was aware I had certain attributes that were not commonly seen among many dark-skinned girls during my era. Growing up with old school ways, being overly criticized, never being allowed to express emotions, I was locked inside myself and having a voice wasn't an option. Being punished was the reward for speaking up so I learned how to be silent.

On top of all of that, I had issues with articulating and enunciating words, expressing my thoughts, and remembering was challenging, especially during stressful situations. It wasn't noticeable, well, at least to the untrained eye but I knew I had trouble learning certain things and I didn't understand why. I wouldn't ask questions for fear of being seen as dumb, thinking others would say, "how can she be pretty and not smart?" So, I was not only conditioned to be silent in the home, I also kept quiet because of social anxiety. I didn't want to be laughed at or teased, so being voiceless became my coping mechanism. Some people think if you are not verbal, engaging or outgoing, you are not intelligent. Society always gravitates towards the worst-case scenario, doesn't it?

Were you ever judged, made to be felt inadequate, or less than? Did it hold you back and keep you from stepping into your power, or had you question your abilities and worth?

Being shy, meek, insecure, naive and lacking confidence wasn't a great start to life. It led me down a road of poor decisions and mistakes. There were so many things I could have avoided, but my deficiencies also introduced me to hardships which showed me that I am *not* breakable or weak, and that I *can* carry the weight of difficulties and be pushed beyond my limitations. I *can* carry on.

Through these adversities, I was shown my strengths and my determination. I was an overcomer, overachiever and a go-getter; all the opposite of what the negative voices told me. I actually had backbone, even though I had been told I didn't. Those who spoke negatively didn't see my capabilities or potential; or maybe they did and thought shaming me would make me improve. Maybe they were projecting their own insecurities and trauma onto me because they knew no other way to communicate themselves. Either way, these were adults, and they chose to focus on my shortcomings and weaponize them against me. But despite the ridicule and harsh words, overcoming my struggles showed me that the labels placed over my head were incorrect. It would take most of my life to see what I overcame through personal development, self-awareness and consistency.

Who is looking at you with judgmental eyes and a negative perception? Who is telling you about all the mistakes they see? Have you had a chance to prove them wrong? Have you had a chance to self-reflect and see all the wonderful things you have inside of you?

Shift Happens

At fourteen years old, my life quickly took a 180-degree turn. I became pregnant. When this happens to a young girl, the assumptions are that she is fast, wild or loose, but none of these were the case. I believed to be in love, but really, I was just an unhappy, unaware teenager looking for love the wrong way. After being dropped off at a juvenile center, brown bag in hand that housed some of my clothes, my new path was in motion. Placement into a group home for unwed mothers and becoming a ward of the state until turning eighteen became my new reality. Talk about "shift happens," this major interruption was completely life transforming. The experience quickly took me out of my television fantasy bubble world of *The Brady Bunch*, *The Partridge Family*, and Doris Day (to name a few), to real-life events that would make your head spin. I had no time to prepare for what was to come. It was a full-body submersion in "The Real Game of Life." I was no longer in Kansas with my dog Toto, but in a whole new world that I had no awareness of. A world I did not grow up knowing or had ever seen on television.

How do I navigate this? I thought.

Before entering this new world order, one of my dreams after graduating high school was to jump in my two-seater Fiat sports car and drive to Paris to be a model. In another imaginary fantasy, I was going to have six kids, a house with a white picket fence (by the age of twenty-six, of course), and a husband who would come home so I could greet him with a martini and cater to his every need. The house would be clean and the kids well-behaved. I would have on a cute dress and pointy-toed heels, as every good "Stepford wife" does. Yeah, crazy … right?

I can laugh at it now, but that was the imagery of realism I had in my head. This was not even the reality I saw in the household I grew up in, but subliminal messaging can do a number on your perception of life, especially if you have been sheltered with a naïve mindset. Disruption has taken place in my life and the truth now was that I was going to have a baby. At that time, I knew nothing about life or myself. I just knew I had to step up and make the best of it to take on responsibilities I was clearly not ready for, nor knew if I could even handle.

I cried every night. I was sorry for what happened. I missed my sister. I wanted to go home. I missed being home, despite the disconnect between me and my mother. I preferred to be home even though I told her I didn't want to be there. At the time, I had no idea what the ramifications of my words would be. I was a teenager going through mental, emotional and physical changes. Kids and teenagers say the craziest things at times in their emotional state, not always realizing the consequences behind some of those choice words or actions. Adjusting to life in an institution was challenging, but it was the start of learning my full capabilities and who I was. Lying beneath my wounds and fears, ready to emerge, were my strength, courage, drive and resilience. I began to overcome the challenges and obstacles placed on my path, showing me there was more to me than I could imagine, much more than just a pretty face.

As I grew older, I would continue to struggle with being naïve, gullible and feeling defeated, but I was learning. I truly had to lead from within to overcome the hardships and survive. There were so many times I wanted to give up, leave my daughter and run off, but I didn't. Despite the odds being stacked against me, I pushed forward and eventually graduated high school at the age of seventeen. This spoke volumes for my determination and intellect, especially since I believed that I wasn't smart. Regardless of this belief, I learned that it's not always about having gifted talent, but the willingness to fight for what you want. I earned accolades as "most improved senior," made the 3.0 honor roll, and was recognized as "best dressed." I also earned a certification in power sewing, learning how to make clothes for myself, my daughter, and doing alterations for others. But truth be told, I really wanted to go into shop class to learn how to wrench cars like the girls on *Duke of Hazards*, who worked on muscle cars wearing daisy dukes. As I mentioned before, the power of subliminal messaging can do you in. Anyway, the school said "no," maybe because I would have been the only girl in class, so I was redirected into sewing. Fashion had already been my first love, so it only cultivated my intrigue for style even more.

While in school I worked a part-time job and took on extra course work to make up credits for failed classes due to poor attendance in ninth grade. The balancing act was far from easy, but this was the start to me being molded into a woman who can take on challenges that life presented. Even though I graduated high school early, I couldn't leave the group home until eighteen. During the summer, through the Unified School District's Youth Summer Program, I was selected to get a job working at Presidio Hospital as a nurse's aide, which was a desirable opportunity. It gave me the idea of wanting to pursue a nursing career, earning a decent wage to provide for me and my daughter. I felt if it meant I had to go to college, I was willing, even though I didn't feel I was college material. I liked the work, assisting at the hospital for veterans; where I made beds, took temperatures, brought food, and helped in whatever way that was needed. I was grateful for the opportunity, skills learned, and income.

Were you ever placed in conditions growing up, where life showed you certain attributes about yourself? Now as an adult, perhaps you now realize there were certain traits you had all along, and it took life experiences to help you see your strengths and limitations. When we are placed in challenging environments, we are forced to push ourselves beyond our limits and discover our truest potential. It is in these moments that we learn the most about ourselves and our capabilities. Will you step up, or fold? Do you take responsibility, or blame others? Do you work hard, or do you look for someone else to take control?

This opportunity to work at the hospital was my second working experience. My first job was working in the kitchen washing dishes at one of the group homes I lived in with my daughter. Having a job was necessary because I only received five dollars a week in allowance for us both. Yes, twenty dollars a month to buy all our needs, clothes, diapers, hygiene products, baby items, etc. And I had no help. The group home provided shelter and three meals a day, and because I was a ward of the state I received a two hundred clothing allowance once a year. So, as you can imagine, working at Presidio Hospital was a dream job.

When the summer program ended, I was saddened but thankful for the experience. The department was unhappy to see me go, as well as the veterans, but it was a temporary job and it was time to move on. At the end, the Unified School District held an assembly for all three hundred kids who worked in their program. They indicated that two kids were going to be given a letter of recommendation, an award of merit and a permanent job at Presidio. Guess whose name was called? Yes, mine and an Asian boy. I was shocked, overjoyed and proud. Out of three hundred kids, I achieved something amazing. I was going to have a permanent position at the hospital, providing a bright future for me and my daughter. I only had to wait a few months before turning eighteen and things were going to be great; I would be leaving the group home with a decent job and a future of possibilities. I was going to work hard and rise through the ranks to become a manager. I had dreams and made plans.

I Had a Dream

Think about all the dreams you had, where you were left heartbroken and disillusioned? Did the dreams seem to crumble? What *is* a dream? A dream is a succession of images, ideas, emotions and sensations that usually occur involuntarily in the mind during certain stages of sleep. A dream takes you out of your current reality, it's an exploration of the possibilities of what can be, especially if you work hard. But what happens when you work hard, and life starts "life'n?" It seemed every time I would get a break or a bit of good news, a wrecking ball would come swinging down to destroy the foundations of what I was trying to build. Nothing was coming easy; everything was a struggle. I would take two steps forward to be thrown three or four steps back. It was depressing, yet I had to keep going.

Once I turned eighteen, I was ready for the job at Presidio Hospital. I reminded myself that this job was awarded to me because of my excellent work ethic, and that gave me a boost of excitement. I was right on the cusp of achieving stability and success for me and my daughter. But in the midst of my excited anticipation, fate dealt a cruel blow. An important message from the hospital was left for me, on the answering machine of my foster mother, and she failed to relay it to me. When I finally contacted the hospital ready to work, it was too late, the opportunity had slipped through my fingers. A dream deferred. I was shattered, livid. That opportunity could have changed the trajectory of my and my daughter's lives. It had given me hope for a bright future, despite how things started off, and now it was gone ... lost, and there was nothing I could do to get it back. My path was redirected, again.

I decided to enroll at a local community college, but after attending classes my insecurities of self-doubt swarmed my thoughts. I believed I wasn't smart enough to succeed academically. My lack of confidence led me to drop out, and once again I embarked on a different path. I sought out six-month training programs to acquire valuable job skills, recognizing that my resilience was my greatest asset (and having a completion date of six months seemed far more attainable than four years). It was during this time that I began to truly understand the "concept" of leading from within. My inner strength had carried me through the darkest of times and it was time to harness it for my journey ahead.

The Lifelong Learner

As an adult I faced numerous challenges, including abusive relationships, homelessness, substance abuse, bankruptcy and divorces. As a single mother of three, life and dreams seemed to be constantly elusive. Despite the darkness threatening to consume me, my inner light refused to be extinguished. Along my journey, various women mentioned a light in my eyes—a quality I never saw myself, because of the hurt, but came to understand as I matured. I knew at times the light I had was dim, flickering because of sorrow, pain and disappointment even to the point of contemplating suicide. But I persisted, fighting to remain strong, continuing to fail forward, despite the difficulties.

Facing turning points, I broke free from hindrances through grueling choices and sacrifices, emerging stronger. Seeking therapy for emotional wounds, I embarked on a journey of self-discovery, learning to recognize my worth and potential. After completing a six-month training program, I secured jobs in law firms and expanded my skills through temp agencies, continuing my journey of personal development. Encouraged by an attorney I worked for, I pushed past my doubts to pursue higher education. Initially resistant, I eventually earned an associate degree, making the honor roll and receiving two academic scholarships to San Francisco State University.

Despite challenges, I obtained bachelor's and master's degrees, while juggling multiple jobs and family responsibilities. Though the attorney who initially motivated me was absent during these achievements, I knew he'd be proud. Statistically improbable, I defied the odds as a teenage mother facing poverty, trauma, abuse, depression, addiction and lack of confidence. My journey exemplifies the power of self-belief and determination. Becoming a Certified Personal & Executive Life Coach, Health Coach and Emotional Intelligence Coach, I use my experiences to inspire others facing adversity. Through my coaching program, UnMaskYourTruth, I assist women in breaking free from self-imposed barriers and embracing a life of empowerment.

Continuing my education, I explore diverse interests on my terms, embracing the spirit of a lifelong learner. My family often wonders if I will ever stop, but my commitment to personal growth allows me to be effective in helping others and my "Dora the Explore" curiosity keeps me inquisitive with learning. Today, I stand as a living testament to leading from within and the power of mindset shifts, illustrating the power of resilience and belief in one's potential.

As a Certified Coach, my practice aims to help women overcome adversity and self-doubt; it lets them see that self-maintenance and personal development is needed for the emotional and mental connection of self. Growth is a continuous journey and at each stage there is a mental maturity that develops which gives us the strength to walk in our power, but we need to unmask, work on the internal maintenance to truly embrace our truth. UnMaskYourTruth empowers women to remove masks, embrace vulnerability, and shift their mindset, allowing them to rise above challenges and step into their power.

My journey, filled with difficulties, trauma and distress, underscores the incredible strength and transformation possible within the human spirit. I hope my story serves as a reminder that, even in our darkest moments, we can find the light within ourselves to guide us toward a brighter future without labels and constraints.

God placed you on your path because he knew certain events in your life needed to shape who you were becoming. Your life events are special to you, it's the path that is going to foster growth, resilience and fortitude. As you walk your journey, remind yourself you have a choice about how you react when adverse situations take control. Pay attention to the opportunities for growth that accompany stressors you will encounter. Growth is the positive change we experience after traumatic events. We cultivate inner strength through the knowledge after overcoming tremendous hardship but if you confront your events and try to make sense of it, it can lead to a powerful mindset shift that will enhance and deepen who you are, and your relationships, so take control of your journey and allow yourself to evolve.

With the ever-changing landscape of life, one thing is certain: shift happens. But remember ... it is not the shift itself that defines us, it's how we choose to respond to it. So, when adversity knocks on your door, dare to answer with unwavering determination and resilience. Embrace change as an opportunity to grow, adapt, and thrive. Don't wait for change to happen to you, instead become the master of your own destiny. Rise above the adversities of life, harness their power, and transform them into steppingstones toward your dreams.

The world is yours to shape, and your story can be an inspiration to others facing their own shifts. Together, let's turn "Shift Happens" into "Shift Empowers." Your call to action begins now; seize the opportunity and let your resilience shine. Change only happens when you decide you want something different, and you want more. Your determination and consistency must be intact. Pushing yourself and being uncomfortable is part of the journey to becoming you. You must take a hard look at yourself every day, fight and fail forward because if you are moving it doesn't matter how long it takes or the mistakes you make. It is the courage you essentially forge through and all the obstacles you must climb to get to where you want to go in life. Sometimes there are no cheerleaders, no support, but you have everything in you to climb that mountain and get to the top.

How bad do you want it? How much are you willing to fight for it? Don't let life or others tell you what you cannot do but show them what you can. Allow your warrior self to emerge triumphant and powerful to defeat anything or anyone that stands in your way. Just like I had to believe in myself, you must believe in you so go out there, grab the world by its balls, look straight into its eyes, squeeze, whisper, *I got this!* Now turn, walk away with confidence … because … *you got this*!

··· ABOUT BRIGGETTE ROCKETT

Briggette Rockett is a personal development expert, personal transformation strategist, wellness advocate, and empowerment coach. With her integrative approach, she empowers women to create sustainable change in their lives, unlock their greatness, tap into their unique gifts, and cultivate a positive mindset. Her unwavering dedication stems from her mission to help women find fulfillment, become unstoppable, and create impact in every area of their lives. As the owner and creator of Rockett Rising LLC, Briggette is a Certified Personal & Executive Life Coach, Health Coach and Emotional Intelligence Coach her established program UnMaskYourTruth assists women in removing the masks of trauma, doubt, and fear, enabling them to overcome negative mindsets and experience a strong desire to transform their lives. Through her work, she guides and supports women, providing the tools and strategies needed to embark on their personal journeys of growth and self-discovery. Briggette's educational background has played a pivotal role in shaping her expertise. She holds a master's degree in education with an emphasis on Instructional Technology. Additionally, she obtained a bachelor's degree in liberal studies with a focus on communication and a minor in counseling.

Website: *www.unmaskyourtruth.com*
LinkedIn: *https://www.linkedin.com/feed*
Facebook: *https://www.facebook.com/Unmaskyourtruth*

16 ··· WHAT WOULD LOVE DO?

by Jackie Cote

It's the darkest challenges that take us to our next level … if we let them.

Each morning I take my dogs out one at a time, so they get alone time with me. They explore in their own ways the smells and beautiful landscape of the Colorado mountains, where my husband and I are parked, living our nomad RV life. It's beautiful during the fall month of November, but the music of the birds has started to dissipate as the weather gets cooler and cooler. But not for two black crows that met me every day on top of the first two trees we walked by each day. They would each fly to the top of their tree and sit there watching me and my dogs walk, as if they were protecting us from above. Once I was on my way back to the RV with the second dog, they would fly away in the same direction every day.

After a few days, I took it as a sign and looked up the meaning of seeing two black crows consistently. I had heard that seeing black crows meant death and that scared me for a moment. What I found was that the number of crows you see has different meanings. Two crows are considered a good omen, symbolizing joy, harmony, upcoming opportunities, and a season of personal growth on the horizon. Of course, this excited me like it would any other "woo woo" girl! Little did I know that I would find out and the big action I would have to take next would be the biggest personal growth I have ever experienced in my life ... and not in the package I ever thought it would come in.

Every Sunday I called my folks to talk to my stepmom and dad, but one day they stopped answering the phone. I left multiple messages but couldn't figure out why there was no answer, or why I couldn't get in touch with anyone to tell me what was going on. So, I called one of my brothers and he told me that my stepmom had been in the hospital for the last month, not able to walk or eat or drink properly, and that a couple of my brothers had been staying with my dad at the house, since he has early onset dementia and couldn't be alone. Without shedding a tear, I subconsciously shifted into my "I got it" mode.

Soon after, I booked a round trip ticket with no change fees, not knowing how long I would be out there to help the situation. I had an "inner knowing" that I would be there for two months. Not sure why that time frame was in my mind, but I knew that was how long I would need to stay. After sharing the news with my husband, I packed my bags and flew to New Jersey to stay on a couch in a cute, but small, retirement home to be my dad's full-time 24-hour-a-day caretaker. Just till things calmed down and my stepmom came home, which we thought we would be sooner than later. Simple, right?

I got this! said my inner "I got it" girl. *I'm great at a lot of stuff so, of course, I will be great at this too. I will save the day!*

Anyone else ever go into this mode immediately? I know I am not alone! But what came next changed my life in ways I could never have imagined. Through this challenging experience I was able to heal wounds, see the lessons, and gain closure on things that were holding me back from my next level in business, relationships and life.

I arrived at the beginning of December and moved my stuff into my dad's house and was ready to go. I got some direction from my brothers about dad's "routine," an address where my stepmom was at in the rehab facility, and that was it. *That's easy, I got this!* I again thought. On the first day of arrival, my brother headed out, the sun went down, and the change began. My dad turned into a man I never knew. He became irritated and frustrated with his sweater and jeans, and then his undergarments. This suddenly changed to an angry conversation about money, regret around his choices, and sadness about my mom, his first love, passing forty-six years ago when I was only five years old.

Uncontrollable tears, shaking, anxiety, which lead to more anger, and he went down a massive rabbit hole about things I never imagined he would say or feel about his life. I was scared, confused, and didn't know what to do as his daughter. I tried to talk him down, and it didn't work. I tried to tell him it would all be okay, and it didn't work. I tried to tell him the things he was feeling weren't true, and it definitely didn't work.

Dad finally laid down but repeatedly yelled that he would die that evening and to be prepared to find him dead. Part of me went numb and thought what the hell did I get myself into? But I quickly kicked back into "I got it" girl mode and called my brother. I put him on speaker to help talk my dad out of the rabbit hole he was in; he had been through this a week earlier and knew how to do it. After an hour or so we calmed him down, redirected him to happier stories, and he came out of the state of rage he was in. What I didn't realize in that moment was he was going through something called sundowning, which is common with dementia patients, especially if they are not getting enough sunlight or vitamin D during their day. It causes them to go deep into an altered state, usually negative, and truly believe in all that they are saying to be true. The rest of the night he stayed awake with short thirty minutes of sleep here and there, and multiple times of getting up to either check his diaper or walk around the house in circles to change the trash, make coffee or do the dishes.

I quickly realized that I would need to be on 24-hour alert for the next six to eight weeks of this journey, for fear of what my dad might do. After a night of no sleep, I wondered if I could do it. But the I Got It Girl kicked back in! *That was one night, I can fix this and make it better. No worries ... I got this!*

The next day was more pleasant while the sun was up, and Dad was more aware of his normal surroundings. He was still obsessing over his bowel movements and not wanting to leak through his diapers and pads so he would use three or four at a time, or fill his diaper with toilet paper and try to convince me that was the best option. Someone told me that when working with a dementia patient, you must be in their world and not deny their truth. This was hard when it was so clearly not the right thing for him. I wanted to control the situation and "fix" it, but instead I let go and leaned into his world. Eventually he calmed down again and we proceeded to enjoy our time together. I took him to a little lake that my stepmom and he would go to before she got sick. We split a turkey sub; each eating only a quarter because it was so huge. We watched the ducks swim, took selfies, and with a stick drew "I love you," in the sand. I was so happy to have this time with my dad, it was a priceless memory I will never forget.

After dinner, the sun went down and like Groundhog Day, the events began to repeat themselves. But this time, I was more prepared and able to stop him from completely going down the rabbit hole, bringing him back quicker. Since I knew it would be another sleepless night, I got my computer out and thought I could get some work done while he watched TV and napped. I thought during his downtime I *should* be able to knock some stuff out. Because you know ... *I got it!* Instead, I sat there on the couch, staring blankly at the computer with tears rolled down my face. I was behind my dad's chair so he couldn't see me, and that was how I wanted it.

Growing up, Dad always had a lot on his plate and didn't have much time for me. It was "okay" because I knew he loved me and was doing what he could to provide for us. So, at a very young age I learned that I shouldn't bother my dad with my fears, challenges, sadness, anger or anything that would cause him more struggles than he already had. I learned how to stuff them down to ignore them and move on. My feelings didn't matter, that was the story that my "little girl self" carried through most of my adult life.

We got through another night, and early the next morning we sat together as he had his cereal and coffee. We talked about how much he missed my mom. He cried as usual, but this time he talked about how much I reminded him of her. How kind, generous, courageous, loving, smart I was—just like her. How people loved her, like people love me. Then he told me how much he loved me and was grateful for *me*. It was those moments that I was beyond grateful for, and yet they also felt awkward. Growing up I never got this kind of one-on-one time with my dad, and I definitely never heard these words out of his mouth to me directly. We just weren't that family to say, "I love you" and, "great job." That moment required great pause to really let myself receive the words, feelings and emotions that he was giving me, without rejecting them.

Five years before this experience I started a journey of real self-development, when I met the coaching world, got fired from my job two months later, and decided to go "all in" on building a coaching business of my own. Little did I know that through the process of building a business, I would discover the deep-down stories—the ones I created to protect myself—that were holding me back from truly loving and owning "me." I had cried the first nine months of working with my first coach, as I healed and released so much. During this time, I learned how to be open to receive what is meant for me. I never realized till that experience with my dad how much I yearned for solo time with him, something I finally received after five decades. Hearing him profess his love, approval and admiration of me was life changing. I knew he loved me, but hearing it opened an inner child wound around abandonment, loss, worthiness and love that was keeping me stagnant in both my life and business. If it wasn't for the work I had done on myself the previous five years, I wouldn't have had the awareness to recognize this wound and the healing it needed.

After breakfast, and he settled into his chair to watch his one of his favorite TV shows, and I went outside and stood in the cold wet grass barefoot and tried to breathe. More tears rolled down my face. I was trying to process the duality of the two-day parts, the receiving of something I was not used to, the lack of sleep, and the fear of not working my business all by myself. After all, I am a coach! I should be able to "handle" this! The next thing I knew I was leaving crying voice messages to my coach about how I can't seem to get any work done in the downtime, and how my dad was so angry. Through tears, I told her all the things I had gone through in the last forty-eight hours. It was early so I knew I wouldn't hear from her till later, but it helped to just get it out, while earthing with the sun on my face and the cool wind drying my tears.

I walked back in after clearing all signs of not being able to handle things, and threw my happy face on to go back to "dad duty." But I came back in a softer version of my typical "I got it" girl. From that day on, I grounded every morning to help ask God for what I wanted, releasing the stress and pain, being grateful for that time, and receiving some inner peace. It became a fun joke with my dad too. He would tell me that I was crazy to go barefoot in the cold December grass, and how he used to be crazy like that when he was young like me. And it became another memory I will never forget with my dad.

My coach got back to me later that day and reminded me of the obvious that I couldn't see. There was no "downtime" in that situation.

When he was settled, I needed to take the time to process all that was happening and emotionally regulate back to neutral the best I could. This was a 24-hour rotation, and there would be almost no time to do work. Money fears started to kick in, but then I remembered why I built my own business in the first place. I could always put family first if needed, and it would be there when I got back. After we finished our call, a good friend called while cooking dinner for my dad.

"I am going to tell you some things that you are not going to want to hear, and you might hang up," he said after I answered. "But I know you, and you need to hear this."

"Okay," I responded, trying to hold back tears.

This is what he said …

1. You think you need to be great at everything, and you aren't … and that is okay.
2. You think you can fix everything, and you can't … dementia is not fixable.
3. You think you must do this alone and not bother anyone … but you can't do this alone. You must ask for help.

It was exactly what I needed to hear in that moment. He was right, even though I didn't want to tell him that! It was time to surrender and give up control of what I *thought* this would be like and lean into what it *was*. Let go and let God.

After shifting my energy and perspective, I asked for help from my brothers to cover dad duty for two to three days at a time for me. I booked a hotel after every ten days just for me to release and recharge so I could be the best version of myself for my dad. After my first break, I came back and things were better. My dad's sundowning became less and less substantial, with the help of a regular routine, supplements and my energy being in a better place. We had more fun and beautifully loving conversations, that I will cherish forever. The "I got it" girl in me was gradually realizing that she doesn't have it all and that is *okay*. And it was time to let go even more. Through asking for help, taking time for self, having a willingness to face pain and challenges, and releasing the false sense of control, I was able to come from a place of trust and love instead of fear and control.

After finally letting go of control, I was able to get my dad amazing assisted living support. God gave me what I asked for and so much more. I then booked some more time for myself at a hotel before coming back to life in Colorado, so I could reflect on all I learned and to reset my energy.

Here are some more lessons I want to share with you.

1. Let go of the need to control this thing called life. It's when we let go and trust that we can truly come from a place of love and create our desires.
2. Let yourself feel the pain and don't stuff it down. Tell someone and get support.
3. Let yourself be aware of the lessons in the challenge. They will help you heal and release the heavy weight you have been carrying for so long.
4. Let yourself receive closure so you can release what is holding you back. You can then rewrite the story to who you truly are and want to experience moving forward.
5. Let yourself love fully and fully be loved. (this just happened for me at fifty years old. Thank you, God!)
6. From all of this you will learn how to love yourself 100 percent inside and out, so you can fully experience what it is like to trust and come from a place of love.

What this challenging experience gave me was the final puzzle piece to my foundation of love. Having a foundation of love will help everything you do to come with more ease and grace. It is what catapults you to your highest levels. It's what will create the most beautiful authentic relationships you have ever experienced. It's what will replace any doubt and fear you have about life. Love is the driving factor to it all.

With love, we are unstoppable!

My mission is to help you complete your puzzle and fully embody the love and light you bring to the world so you, too, can feel unconditional self-love and be unstoppable! It's time to shift from the "I got it" girl. who has learned she must be in control and do it all by herself, to the new "*we got it, girl!*" who trusts she is fully supported and loved unconditionally.

You are never alone because I am here by your side, my friend.

Much love to you!

⋯ ABOUT JACKIE COTE

I'm Jackie, your Freedom and Love Mentor and owner of Jackie Cote Coaching. I help you shift from the "I got it!" girl who is in control from a place of fear to the woman who lets go, trusts and knows that love will lead the way to the life of freedom she truly loves.

I'm a Jersey girl at heart but haven't lived there since the nineties. Instead, I have been a traveling spirit for the last thirty years creating my version of a Freedom life. In 2018 I got fired and decided to finally bet on me and go for it! I built my online coaching business which gave me the freedom to jump in a RV and live the nomad life to travel the country with my husband and two pups living life on my terms.

My mission is to help 100k or more women to Awaken, Empower and Own their magic so they can create purpose driven lives where they feel loved, alive and free every day!

Website: *www.jackiecotecoaching.com*
Facebook: *https://www.facebook.com/jackie.j.cote*
Instagram: *https://www.instagram.com/jackiecotecoaching*
LinkedIn: *https://www.linkedin.com/in/jackie-cote-59a404190*

17 ··· REDISCOVERING

PURPOSE

by Karen Rae

Amidst the turbulence of life's storms, I found myself grappling with a profound and pressing question that seemed to echo through the chaos. How do we unearth our purpose and hold onto our sense of visibility when it feels like the very fabric of our existence is unraveling? It was a question that weighed heavily on my heart as I embarked on a transformative journey, a quest to craft a new and beautifully meaningful life amid the relentless tides of uncertainty and chaos.

In the midst of circumstances that lay far beyond my control, I was thrust into the pot of uncertainty, gripped by fear, and faced with the agonizing disintegration of dreams and plans that had once formed the very core of my existence. For the longest time, I had lived the life I thought I desired, a life I had built with my family. I felt an inner drive to fight to preserve our bond and to prevent our family from fracturing. I knew I had to stand up for my values, and for what I believed in, and most importantly, I had to reclaim my power—allowing my inner light and unique gifts to shine forth while rediscovering my inner beauty. Through this transformative journey, I've unearthed three beautiful pillars of wisdom that have stood as unwavering guides throughout my life. I've shared these insights as I navigate life's trials, and I continue to hold them close as they illuminate my path forward.

Let's journey back to where it all began, to the narrative I had woven for myself. During that time, life appeared to be ideal. I was preparing for a new season in life as my children were on the cusp of leaving the nest, and my family and I were discovering what lay beyond. We lived in a charming home nestled within a golf course community, brimming with laughter, shared moments, and the joy of witnessing our children's growth. For twenty-seven years, I had been a dedicated stay-at-home mom, cherishing the bustling days spent with my family—filled with sun-soaked boat trips, adventures on Whidbey Island, winter escapes to the mountains for skiing, and getaways to Cabo and Cancun. Weekends were marked by delightful dinners with cherished friends and family. I treasured every aspect of my life, believing that we had a strong marriage and a thriving family.

We had, indeed, weathered numerous storms over the years, including the challenges of our children's health and other hurdles that, in my eyes, had only strengthened the bonds within our family and marriage. I fondly expressed gratitude for the wonderful life we were building together. I remember those car rides, sharing tales of our seemingly charmed life and what I believed was a great marriage. We'd compare ourselves to others, blissfully unaware of the truth lurking beneath the surface. Those little nagging doubts, the odd comments that I brushed aside, telling myself I shouldn't rock the boat. Looking back now I realize that I had lost my voice, afraid to make waves.

One day, I found myself sitting on the edge of the bed, folding clothes, questioning my purpose and my unsettled feelings about my marriage. It was a moment of reckoning, a time to look within. With a hopeful heart, I took proactive steps and reached out to a counselor, believing that I had identified the root cause of my struggle: a sense of purposelessness, as I navigated the transition into a new chapter of my life. Simultaneously, I was crafting a community of women, a haven I named "Fave," where we celebrated all things women love and want to share with their girlfriends. My husband was embarking on a new job, traveling the world, and my kids were growing up. So, I dabbled in a new hobby—creating short YouTube videos.

With my kids' assistance, we set up a camera and started my vlog to showcase all the things women love along with their stories and experiences. *Why not create a show and invite some girlfriends and film at the local wineries?* I thought. I approached one of my favorites, asking if I could film there and invite friends. The idea blossomed into an event, and forty-five women eagerly attended the first Fave filming. I had never done anything like it before, but it was such a hit that I began reaching out to other wineries and captivating women for interviews on various lifestyle topics. Unbeknownst to me, I was slowly carving out a new purpose for myself, and I eventually stopped seeing the counselor, believing I had found my way—a new purpose.

As the months passed, I tiptoed around what I believed was the problem, perhaps in denial, lacking the courage to confront the strange feelings. I clung to the hope that we could weather the storm, as we had in the past—job pressures, travel and the challenges of raising children. But fate had other plans. The night my husband asked me to bring a box of tissues for our talk, I crumbled like a child, unable to articulate my emotions. Throughout my life, I have allowed others to speak for me, giving away my power to avoid criticism or the fear of being misunderstood. I was often labeled as too sensitive or too defensive, so I often chose to stay silent to avoid confrontation with more outspoken individuals.

When my husband left, fear gripped me. My thoughts went to the worst-case scenarios I could imagine, as I created stories in my head of being homeless, or asking myself, who would hire a twenty-seven-year stay-at-home mom at the age of fifty-eight? I felt devoid of marketable skills, my self-worth in tatters, betrayed, abandoned, and in despair. But there was a divine plan at play.

I'm a woman of faith, and slowly, incredible people entered my life and believed in me. Little did I know that I was already on a path to rediscovering myself through a passion project called Fave. It wasn't started as a business but as a gathering place for women, a place where someone acknowledged that I was alive and making a difference by creating special moments for them to shine. Here, I didn't have to take a backseat. I cherished being a mother, but as my kids transitioned into adulthood and my husband's work and travel took precedence, our marriage suffered and I felt pushed to the fringes. I had become a checklist, a taskmaster, feeling like nothing I did was ever perfect or enough. Yet, I could create beauty at these events, where women came together, had fun, and thanked me for providing a space to meet new friends.

Throughout my journey, my strength came from my faith and seeing God's hand in the people he surrounded me with. A friend challenged me to come from a place of love even in the most trying of times, others reminded me of how God saw me, with comforting words and believing I had value outside of marriage or being a mom. It was this unwavering faith and the profound belief in my worth that provided the foundation for my transformation.

With divorce looming on the horizon, my life, the one I had known for over half of my adult years, was undergoing a seismic shift overnight. My financial security, my cherished family home—everything—was in flux.

At fifty-eight years of age, I found myself abruptly facing the daunting task of starting anew, all on my own. My identity as a wife, mother, friend and member of a family was undergoing a profound transformation. It was time to embark on a journey of self-discovery, to redefine my personal worth and to discover who I truly was.

During the two challenging years of dissolving my marriage, I vividly recall a pivotal moment in counseling. My therapist asked me to write down how I saw myself in my marriage and life. I wrote a single word: invisible. It hit me like a lightning bolt as he had written the same word on his piece of paper. All those years of being a wife and mother, I had become invisible in my own life, losing sight of myself. It was time for a change; I needed to treat myself as visible and unearth my hidden gifts. I realized the adventure was only just beginning, with so much left to discover. I committed to focus on myself, to navigate the trails of my divorce with as much grace and dignity as I could muster up, and to choose joy and positivity as my guiding lights.

I also learned that asking for help was not a sign of weakness but a path to surround myself with incredible people who could guide me in positive ways. I granted myself an hour each day to feel anger, cry, fear and frustration. *Just* an hour. The rest of the day was dedicated to rebuilding myself and crafting a new life. Following my life coach's advice, I wore a rubber band to snap my thoughts back to self-care whenever my mind wandered into negative territory. It took practice but I learned to prioritize self-care. I discovered how I wanted to be treated and mastered the art of saying "no."

My girlfriends were my pillars of strength during this trying time. One dear friend sent me a daily text—a note of encouragement or a bible verse. Sometimes, a simple text meant the world. I gave myself the grace to learn to stand on my own and to open my heart, coming from a place of love. I also dedicated time to embrace new perspectives, to pause and respond rather than react, to savor the present moment, and to understand that forgiveness is a process. I realized that joy is a choice, and I learned to love others where they are without adding unnecessary stories to their actions. The lessons seemed endless, and the journey had only just begun. There is so much curiosity left in life to discover.

Amidst the chaos, I discovered my value, and my worth, and built a new, healthier identity filled with vibrancy, love and trust. I learned the importance of living in the moment, of embracing vulnerability and authenticity, reaching out for help, and serving others in a healthy capacity. I embarked on a journey of learning to trust my God-inspired intuition, seeking guidance for the path ahead. Initially, I clung to what was familiar, the life I had once known and thought I wanted. But the universe had different plans. While I initially believed I was fighting to preserve the family unit, I soon realized that my attention needed to shift inward, towards myself. I needed to cultivate vibrancy within myself and take courageous steps forward. My focus shifted towards monetizing my passion project, Fave

I had garnered a modest social following and observed women entrepreneurs flourishing at the events I hosted. So, I ventured into the world of online entrepreneurship, launching a magazine featuring content from these incredible women. Simultaneously, I continued to host quarterly events, providing a platform for others to showcase their brilliance. This platform offers three important pillars for transformation.

This became my primary pillar—choosing to show up. I made the conscious choice to show up as my authentic self, sharing my vibrant energy and realizing that this was more than enough. I became acutely aware of the freedom that came with shedding the need to conform to others' expectations. This shift wasn't immediate, and I often had to remind myself of this foundational principle as I navigated my roles as an entrepreneur, businesswoman, and newly single woman, encountering new challenges along the way. One such challenge emerged when the world was hit by a pandemic, threatening to disrupt my newly established business, focused on connecting women. In-person events were halted, and I was compelled to relocate from my local area due to my altered financial circumstances as the head of a single household. In response, I chose to show up virtually, going live five days a week to engage with the women in our community. Our online community flourished during this period as women sought connection through digital means.

Amidst these trials, I unearthed my overarching mission—to Celebrate One Million Women, fostering a community grounded in abundance, generosity, and a genuine commitment to uplifting others and allowing their unique gifts to shine. It occurred to me that if I had once felt invisible, without a space to have a voice or share my gifts, I could create that space for others. This mission breathed purpose into my life, allowing me to serve others, much as I had done during my marriage and while raising my family.

During this period, I came to understand the power of education, which emerged as the second pillar of my transformation. I embarked on a journey to educate myself in various domains, recognizing that knowledge held the key to empowerment. I began by attending workshops on business management and relentlessly scoured all the free resources. At times, the sheer volume of information seemed overwhelming, particularly as I grappled with my perceived lack of technical, financial and sales expertise needed to realize my goals. Nevertheless, with each tentative step I took, I found a bit of self-assurance that propelled me forward. I dedicated myself to learning about my deepest fears, honing life skills, understanding the intricacies of building a business, and envisioning the life I truly desired. With support, I transformed my vision into a tangible reality—a platform where women could access these invaluable resources at Fave.

Education became synonymous with empowerment; it breathed life into my confidence and instilled a profound sense of self-worth. Through education, I discovered new horizons and remained steadfast on the path of defining who I am and what I want in life, continuing my journey of self-discovery.

One of the most profound moments in this transformative journey was when my son approached me one day, saying, "Mom, I have a gift for you." This singular gesture would resonate deeply within me, marking a pivotal turning point. He bestowed upon me the Gift of Opportunity—an invitation to explore the limitless possibilities that life had to offer. This remarkable act fundamentally reshaped my perspective. Not only did I come to realize that I possessed the agency to navigate this new chapter of my life, but I also consciously chose to traverse this path with strength and courage. Even though I stumbled along the way, at times, more times than I could count, my objective remained clear: to emerge from this turbulent period as a whole and healthy individual. It was during this phase that the true significance of the second pillar—education—fully came to light. With the Gift of Opportunity came an abundance of possibilities and a chance to broaden my horizons. Education evolved into a beacon of hope and empowerment on my ongoing journey of self-discovery and transformation.

My third and final pillar revealed itself as the importance of surrounding myself with remarkable people who not only inspired me to seek the positive but also nurtured my growth and encouraged me to become a source of inspiration by sharing my story. Through this journey, I was fortunate to welcome life mentors who entered my world, shedding light on a broader perspective, fostering a focus on what could be, and, most significantly, believing in me.

Believing in someone, as I discovered through these remarkable mentors, transcends mere encouragement. It's a profound act of faith in a person's potential, an unwavering belief in their ability to rise above challenges and evolve into their best selves. These mentors worked closely with me, guiding me on the path of forgiveness, teaching me to establish healthy boundaries, and helping me claim my standards. They encouraged me to find my voice, to show up as Karen, the person I had once been but had gradually lost sight of. I distinctly remember when a friend said, "Karen, you used to be so vibrant, and then you got lost, and now you are back." It was a poignant realization that I had lived up to others' expectations for so long that I had lost touch with my true self. The fear of rediscovering the real "Karen" was daunting, as I wasn't certain whether I would even like her. During this process, I encountered the painful reality of severed relationships with family and friends. It was then that I resolved to approach this self-discovery journey with curiosity and to find the pieces of myself that I genuinely liked.

Two of the most important people who believed in me came from my sons, who shared their wisdom, encouragement and love throughout this transformative journey. Their unwavering support and belief in my capacity to overcome challenges bolstered my determination. It was their reminders of how God saw me, not solely as a wife or mother, but as a woman with intrinsic value, that kept me moving forward. Their words were a beacon of hope, reinforcing the idea that my journey was about creating a beautiful life from the pieces I had left and the ones I was still discovering.

In this quest, I began to derive joy from life's simple pleasures, to be fully present in the moment, and to savor meaningful interactions with friends. The wisdom of the remarkable women who had become my pillars continued to illuminate my path. Their generosity in helping me navigate life, their willingness to challenge me to step out of my comfort zone, and their unwavering belief in my potential moved me to tears. I am immeasurably blessed by the opportunity to share my story with all of you, as someone who believed in me enough to provide this platform for me to express myself. I hope that you, too, will encounter individuals who believe in you as fervently as they did in me, for it is through such belief that we find the strength to rise, transform and inspire others in return.

Through the three pillars of rediscovering my purpose, embracing education as a source of empowerment, and surrounding myself with remarkable mentors and women who believed in me, I've emerged not only stronger but also as my more authentic myself. It's been a journey of peeling back the layers and revealing the woman I always was but had lost sight of along the way.

As I reflect on where I started—feeling invisible and lost—and where I am now—standing in the light of my own authenticity and purpose—I can only describe the feeling as incredible. I no longer see myself as invisible; I've become a vibrant, capable and visible individual. This journey has reshaped the very core of my being, one walked with courage and vulnerability, learning and growing at every step. I have learned that life's challenges are not obstacles but opportunities for profound growth, each trial a stepping stone along the path of self-discovery. I hope my story serves as inspiration, resonating with your experiences and encouraging you to embrace your uniqueness, believe in your potential, and welcome the boundless possibilities life offers.

Your story, too, is waiting to be written with an open heart and unwavering self-belief.

··· ABOUT KAREN RAE

Hello, I'm Karen Rae, the founder of Fave, a vibrant membership community dedicated to creating an extraordinary experience for visionary female entrepreneurs and founders. My journey into creating Fave was inspired by a series of unexpected life challenges, including divorce, re-entering the workforce after 27 years as a stay-at-home mom, living independently for the first time, and navigating the transitions of becoming an empty nester and going through menopause. In the face of these challenges, I made a conscious decision not just to survive but to thrive, to shine brightly in my own life, and to create a space where other women could join in celebrating their journeys, connecting with like-minded individuals, and fostering personal and professional growth.

At Fave, we are on a mission to redefine how women connect, emphasizing values like generosity, abundance, and a shared commitment to making a positive impact in the world. To enhance our community's connectivity and support, we've recently launched the New Fave Girlfriends Network App, designed to ignite growth while facilitating meaningful connections among our members.

Website: *www.favelifestyles.app*
Instagram: *https://www.instagram.com/favelifestyles*
Facebook: *https://www.facebook.com/FaveLifestyles*

18 ··· NAKED, RAW ...AND REAL

by Toni Burbridge

There have been many spaces in my life where intuition kicked in and I either listened to it, or I swallowed it—pushing it down, ignoring it, and denying its voice.

From a very early age, I heard the calling; a distinct familiar voice that was not my own. My story is one of leaning in and trusting. Choosing one aspect to highlight where it's changed the trajectory of my life has turned into a series of instances and events of leaning in and trusting the voice— the Holy Spirit, the voice of God, and my own internal compass. My intuition has become the basis of where I am today.

My peace is absolutely non-negotiable now. Why is that, you ask? My story is one of chaos to kingdom. Most of my life was littered with chaos. Chaos internally, which reflected externally. Or was this the conditioning of my entire upbringing? Growing up lower middle class, I was raised by a single mother who worked three jobs, with a father who disappeared after the divorce. We were latchkey kids; eight and nine years old thrown into adulthood. I cared for my mother from the age of nine to thirty-eight, when she passed at fifty-eight years young from diabetic complications. At the time, I was a single mother of twins trying to break out of the welfare system, to be something more for my daughters.

The *chaos* was daily!

Chaos cluttered my home, my mind, my heart and literally bled out onto every aspect of my life, like dirty sludge covering, thick and murky, hard to navigate. I could not move! I felt as though I was suffocating. Chaos was suffocating my life, my career, my family and what I wanted to do in the world. My life was so messy. Yet, I still clung to just a smidge of hope.

Fairly early in my career, I made a leap into the contracting and consulting world, which was scary, as I'd worked at the same company for eight years. However, I was miserable, and after my mother's death I could not financially sustain with a non-profit income. So, I made a leap and instantly doubled my income.

Finally, I can breathe, I had thought. *I am getting stable and gaining my footing after my mother's death.*

There were a lot of complexities, turmoil and chaos between my mother and me. After she had passed, I was content with where my life was heading. My twins were about to turn fourteen. My side business was starting to gain some traction. However, one of my girlfriends wanted to play matchmaker. Welcome to more *chaos!*

"Nah, I am good with where I am right now. I don't need nor want the complications of dating," I told her.

About a week after this conversation with my girlfriend, I received a Facebook message from a man. At that time, I didn't connect with people I didn't know personally. Once we'd exchanged a few messages, as I was trying to place where I knew him, I sighed and rolled my eyes as I realized he was the man my friend wanted me to meet. We started talking over the phone, and his smooth buttery voice got me. We started talking every day. Two weeks later, we met for dinner. It was a blind date for me as he had no picture on Facebook—this should have been my first red flag. Dinner was pleasant, he had flowers in the car for me after dinner, stating he had not brought them in but saved them for if I "deserved" them, which I had thought was odd. There are so many things I look back on now that I would not have done. Hindsight is 20/20 after all.

Things progressed over the next few months. However, there was something unsettled in the pit of my stomach, there were little things that didn't add up. Within a couple of months, a woman showed up at his house banging on the door. He rapidly pulled me to the bathroom. After the banging stopped, he left for work. I peeked out the window, she was yelling at him, smacked him in the back of his head, continued yelling, and pointing her finger in his face.

"I'm gonna get you for child support!"

I was so perplexed. Child support? He told me he was single and not seeing anyone. He called and told me to stay in the house, saying that she was crazy and would be waiting outside, then explained the rest away. This was one of many instances that I allowed to transpire. The rest were inconsistencies in stories and patterns, and the level of gaslighting was very real.

Here's the thing I ignored: I knew within the first three months that I needed to cut this relationship off. The insane part is I was trying to prove a point to myself that I could be in a relationship, and I tried to make it work for eleven years. I pushed down my own voice and intuition multiple times a day that told me to leave. I would tell myself; it will get better. So, cliché! There were small pockets of time where things between us would be better. He'd be kind, semi-attentive, we'd go away on trips, and have nice dinners together. But then it would go back to the same. He would wane hot and cold, not touch me for months, leaving me wondering what I had done, and whether I was even loved. He'd twist my words and tell me that I didn't see what I saw. He'd say things like, "Are you going to put on some makeup? You look rough like a biker chick." I would walk on eggshells, twist and turn to be what I thought he wanted. The reality was he didn't know what he wanted, nor what he had.

I separated from him as soon as I knew he was with someone else, while telling me he wasn't, it came out later that indeed he was entertaining someone else. During that time, I had an urgency ... a push ... a feeling to visit a church I had attended many times in the past. I listened, and in doing so, the day I walked back into church was the day I met the woman who became my coach. I watched from my seat as this radiant beacon of peace, light and love as she resigned her position to go out on her book tour. What I saw emanating from her is what I so desperately needed in my life.

I saw *joy!*

Even amid all the turmoil, I started working with this coach in a life transformation program. I worked with her for five years. Doing the inner work on myself and trusting the process I began to rebuild my voice. In the coaching program, I developed deep, rich and connected relationships with women. I didn't know how much my soul needed other women I could grow with, cry with, and elevate beside to each new level. What I gained within her coaching program is lifelong sisterhood, women who have permission to not only check on me but to check me when I am veering off course. I trust these women implicitly with my deepest confidences, my visions, and the cultivation of my life. They have walked with me through some of my darkest places and celebrated with me at the apex of each triumph.

My ex and I reconciled after only six months of separation, but it didn't take long for the same old patterns to transpire. And towards the end of our relationship, I nearly hit a bicyclist. I was so distracted, so unhappy, so empty inside that my mind was elsewhere. In the same month, we took a trip. It was a trip I knew I should have declined. My mind was so chaotic and still so distracted, I literally hit a wall. I stood turned and walked so fast, I walked straight into the edge of an RV pullout. I hit my head so hard, instantaneously I dropped to my knees because I instinctively knew I would pass out if I did not. I was there for several moments when he came around the corner because I wasn't responding to the task at hand.

"What are you doing?" he asked.

"I'm not okay!" I yelled as I crouched on the ground. There was no answer, so I yelled again.

"I'm not okay!"

"Why are you yelling?" he asked, as he came around to look at me. I knew it was bad by the look on his face.

"Let's get you inside and get some ice on that," he said.

When I finally looked—about thirty minutes later—I had a lump about two inches long, an inch wide, and about a quarter of an inch raised. My only thought at the time was, *I hope all these folks out here know the signs of concussion*, as I went back to sleep.

Today, I still have a small lump on my head as a reminder of where I have come from. That day was a turning point for me; not only did I physically hit a wall, but figuratively as well. I entered two months of turmoil and stress, gaining thirty pounds in about six weeks. I was completely empty inside. My smile and laughter were gone, my eyes were hollow. I was a shell of the woman he'd met.

The day I decided to leave, I was driving around, praying, feeling the tightness in my chest, thinking and I heard the voice again.

"It's time to leave."

I drove to his house with the tiniest amount of love I had left for myself and ended the relationship. In that moment, I became a *warrior!* Little did I know how much longer it would take to untangle everything. It has taken years.

Looking back, each time I stepped away and recovered my footing, focused on myself and what I desperately wanted and needed in the relationship, I gave it to myself. But that is when elevations occurred. When I was not navigating the minefields of gaslighting, breadcrumbing, mental and emotional abuse, I flourished. Not only did I elevate my stability in my own self, but I would also elevate and stabilize in my career and income. Each time my career and income took a leap upward. And every time I stepped back into the situation, I was again bombarded with negativity, self-doubt and at times led to feel as if I was crazy—as that was the narrative that he would feed me, and I swallowed it. I now know I am a survivor of narcissistic abuse and very recently I have navigated post-separation abuse too.

I was attending a retreat a few years ago. I awoke on a Sunday morning to the beauty and warmth of the Arizona desert. I so needed this retreat as my life was still in somewhat of a chaotic state. That morning, we were instructed not to speak from the time we woke until breakfast. We did morning stretching on the lawn before our silent walk. As I walked the grounds of the Royal Palms Resort and Spa, I relished in the beauty, the birds singing filled the air as the sun kissed my skin. The peacefulness of the early morning drenched the atmosphere around us. I prayed, walked silently, then found my place by the pool, as the sound of the fountains brought peace and stillness in my soul. Drinking in the sunshine as I continued to pray and listen, until I heard the distinct and clear instructions.

"Sell your house."

"Lord, are you crazy?" I asked.

But I heard it again.

"Sell your house."

No other instructions were given. I shared about it at the retreat and when I returned home, shared about it again with my manager.

"Okay, so when are you starting?" he asked.

I was still financially recovering from the year prior and had a large unemployment gap from the instability I'd experienced. I was "robbing Peter to pay Paul" as my mother would say. It was only by the grace of God that I survived that period. But it was time to roll up my sleeves and start the work on the house. It was an enormous task and at times absolutely exhausting. There was a lot of chaos and turmoil that lay within those four walls. Even though my mother had passed many years prior, she had been a hoarder and the house was still full of her belongings. I was a tired single mother with no help, going between my ex's and my house for years, that I just did not have the time nor energy to tackle it alone. Chaos upon chaos, upon chaos. There were many times I cried from the overwhelm.

This was the beginning of the biggest purge of my life, and I started where I could. I began listing and selling items. I made multiple runs to the dump and eventually narrowed down everything in that house—forty-seven years' worth—into one U-Haul Pod, which is the equivalent of one and a half rooms. I narrowed it even further to their smallest tow behind trailer. With each item sold, thrown out and given away, I gained more of myself back. It was as though a weight that I cannot describe lifted, and my internal and external territory was regained. It made room for me to make the biggest leap of my life to date.

I sold my house and paid off debt. I was defrauded during this time as I wasn't leaning in and listening to my own internal voice, *again*. I stayed in Washington state nine months longer than I had intended. There was still turmoil present in an internal struggle to fully release everything I was instructed to release. My ex was still popping up. I was still trying to navigate the feelings of my grown children and my own guilt of how I had not been fully present with them physically and emotionally as they grew and developed. And I still knew that to become who I was purposed to be, I had to release *all* that I knew, *all* that I had, *all* that I was, and *all* that others expressed I should be. I began the release.

I packed up the 4'x8' trailer with mostly essentials with the help of my brother and we drove nearly three thousand miles across the United States. In three days, we crossed eight states, slept twice at friends' homes, and landed in North Carolina at night. It was warm that September evening, as we pulled up to the Airbnb. As I walked up the porch, I saw a scurry.

"What was that?" I asked my brother.

"What was what?" he responded.

We went in and looked around, and as we were about to go unload the car for the evening, across the floor we saw another roach scurry. Well, that Airbnb stay stopped that instant. I filmed the scurry outside as they were there again. Long story short there, they refunded my stay. Which led to my staying and renting from a woman I had only met in a mastermind five years prior. She and I had remained in contact. This was another moment of leaning in and listening to my internal voice to contact her. It's been an incredibly deep and beautiful friendship we've developed. And it also led to my learning that there are great women that can be trusted. She genuinely loves me and cares about me. It was a healing experience that I wasn't anticipating. The healing was not only her presence in my life but the beautiful peaceful space of the Farm. I've always cared for and looked out for others, to have someone do the same for me was something I had not really experienced and from a virtual stranger. This woman even took care of me when I was sick, making homemade soups and juices. Her love and kindness, I will never forget.

For my birthday a few months after moving in at the Farm, I was invited to Charlotte, NC, by another woman I had been introduced to by one of my coaches, prior to my leaving Washington state. I went to stay with her for a week while we celebrated my birthday. As I prepared to head back home, she stated she didn't want me to leave because she enjoyed my company so much. I proposed that I rent from her. And once again, a virtual stranger opened her home to me. I rented from her for a year. We developed a deep and amazing friendship as well. Again, a woman, a virtual stranger became a lifelong friend. She also brought deep healing by sharing stories, wisdom and opening her heart and home.

All this to say, leaning in and listening to my internal voice—to my intuition and the voice of God—has led me to places I never thought I would be. If anyone had told me six years ago that I would sell my house and move to North Carolina, I would have said they were crazy. At the time, I was still in a relationship going nowhere, in a house I hated, in a state I hated, in a life I hated, but could not see a way out of, or how to change the circumstances. It was through the release of what I thought was going to be the rest of my life. It was taking a hard look at my life then embracing and truly feeling into the possibilities. It was allowing women to surround me and midwife my visions, my hopes, my dreams and challenge me to release the angst, the dreariness of my life to expand my wings to soar and become the woman God created me to be.

What I have learned about myself in the last fifteen years is that I am a beacon of hope. I am light. I am inspiration. I live my life out loud, and others are watching and inspired. I am a trailblazer, and I have only begun. I am excited for these next fifty years of my life, as I have just gotten started. Because I am love and loving with an open heart, I see more beauty in people, places and things. I have immense gratitude and thankfulness for all that has transpired for the entirety of my life as it's made me who I am. Chaos still tries to rear its ugly head here and there, but what I have discovered is I am much less tolerant of those things that would once have disrupted my peace, because my peace is absolutely non-negotiable.

Since I have released all the things that were blocking me—including people, places and things—I have gained so much. I have come full circle by becoming healthier and through healing: spiritually, mentally, emotionally, physically and in my relationships. I now live in a beautiful space that I wrote about five years ago that's a leap pad to owning a home again, but on my own terms. I have been financially stable for three years now and my income has increased nearly 4000 percent since my worst financially chaotic crisis. I smile, laugh and sing often, as well as have deep peace and joy. These are all things that I had lost in the chaotic and toxic relationships. And this is just the beginning of my story of Chaos to Kingdom.

I believe in radical ownership of my life by accepting the parts I played and allowing space for forgiveness and growth. Letting it all go became the planting ground for my growth. I now help executive level, c-suite, and entrepreneurial women to breakthrough and unapologetically, authentically, genuinely and lovingly own who they are, to make the leap and navigate their next great adventure.

··· ABOUT TONI BURBRIDGE

Toni Burbridge emerges as a dynamic, inspiring, and intuitive leader with over fifteen years studying healing modalities. Her journey from overcoming welfare to achieving significant financial success exemplifies the power of determination and self-discovery.

As a coach and healer, Toni empowers her clients to navigate life's intricate challenges and make transformative leaps forward. With a keen ear for the unspoken and a gift for uncovering deeper truths, Toni offers profound wisdom to illuminate paths to greatness. She guides individuals to embrace their unique life's purpose with unwavering confidence and clarity.

With an unparalleled blend of wisdom and holistic healing practices cultivated throughout her own transformative journey, Toni radiates a magnetic energy that invites others to join her in embracing a life filled with boundless joy, profound love, and infectious laughter. Her mantra, "Dare to Live a Life Overflowing with Joy, Love, and Laughter," serves as a beacon of hope and possibility for all who encounter her.

Website: *www.toniburbridge.com*
LinkedIn: *www.linkedin.com/in/toniburbridge*
Linktree: *https://linktr.ee/toniburbridge*

19 ⋯ BROKEN OPEN

by Venita Qualls

I have never written about my life experiences before, but I would love to tell you how good God has been to me. I was raised in foster care from six months old until being legally adopted at sixteen. I was born to a sixteen-year-old teenage girl and eighteen-year-old teenage boy, both too young to know what life was all about for themselves, never mind how to raise a baby.

My father was the oldest of nine children and lived in Boston with his mother. My mother was the oldest of four and lived forty miles away from Boston. My mother would travel to Boston for work, and I would stay with a babysitter. As the story goes—as there are other versions—as time went on, my mother's presence slowly decreased and then stopped, and I ended up staying at the babysitter's house. At six months old, I became a ward of the state of Massachusetts. My babysitters became my foster parents—my

God sent parents, —and at seventeen years old, they adopted me. They didn't have to "take me in," but they did, and I love them for it. I love and miss my parents so much and thank them from the bottom of my heart for their love, empathy, compassion, self-sacrifice, and humanity for helping people that couldn't help themselves—my biological mother, father and *me!* My life experiences from then until now, more than fifty years later, has taken me full circle to my life's purpose of helping others and doing what I do. So, what do I do?

I am a licensed mental health and licensed addiction counselor. I had aspired to become a CEO of a Fortune 500 company, or something of that nature when I was in my late twenties. I often thought about becoming an entrepreneur but didn't know what business to focus on and there was no one in my family who had a business to learn from. I had no mentors, no guides. Little did I know that a major life event would change my life forever. It would turn my world upside down and life, as I knew it, would change. I would never be the same again. This change would open up my world to losing everything, but also to gaining everything. A life of self-renewal, soul-mending and service providing. From pain to purpose.

Once upon a time, I had a stable job. I attended college and obtained both my bachelor's and a master's degrees, and I bought a condominium. I thought I had "arrived." I worked hard to get where I was during this time in my life, but life as I knew it was about to change. All the hard work I did in the prior years was about to crumble right before my eyes. I lost my house due to foreclosure during the 2008 housing crash. The adjustable-rate mortgage came due one day, and I couldn't afford the payment. I filed for bankruptcy and a year later it was discharged. My debts were cleared but my credit fell, and it took years to rebuild it again.

Shortly after, I was arrested for an OUI charge (operating under the influence of alcohol). A year later, I picked up a second OUI charge—after pleading out my first charge—as well as driving with a suspended license.

Because of my cases, I chose to resign from my court career in the probation department. My life had become such a mess.

I was broken open!

My heart, my soul, my whole being was disrupted and dismantled. I was in a lot of pain, both mentally and spiritually, and I didn't even know how damaged I was. I was depressed and didn't know how to recognize the symptoms. As I think back to my symptoms of depression, I experienced a lack of interest in things I enjoyed, I had sleep disturbance, I cried for no reason, I had a change in my appetite, poor concentration, and suicide ideations. I thought to myself, *what are you going to do about this?*

I was *broken open*; wide open. I was lost and dead—soul dead. I was all alone and didn't know what to do.

I had other disappointing events happen to me during my lifetime, but I continued through life as if nothing had happened and kept moving. I never stopped to access myself. I never thought these past experiences and events were considered trauma. I thought I was fine until I was broken open, and all the hurt and pain started to show up in my actions and behaviors. It wasn't until after the second OUI case that I checked myself into a mental health facility for major depressive disorder.

In Massachusetts, under the Melanie Law, driving with a suspended license under an OUI carries a mandatory one-year jail sentence, so my charges sent me to jail. This is where I began my deep relationship with God. When you are in jail, the administration provides a Bible to their guests. You may have heard that people find God in jail. Well, it's true. There is nothing else to do but read, so why not read the Bible? I was being held at a women's prison called MCI Framingham, and I was awaiting transfer to the Women in Transition program—also known as WIT, a county sheriff's pre-release program. This was the beginning of my life's journey and life changing events.

The first book I read in the Bible was Ecclesiastes Chapter 1:1-9. King Solomon talks about how there is nothing new under the sun. Everything that has been done on earth has been done many times before. Ecclesiastes captured my heart and soul. *Oh my God!* I thought to myself. I was absolutely mesmerized and finished reading it in just a few hours. I needed a word. I needed to fill my soul with good words because I had been defeated. Life had caught up to me and I was *broken open*! I had fallen and couldn't get up, at least not by myself. I needed help and the only one who could save me was God. I continued reading the Bible and began learning about what God wanted for his people—and for me.

Prior to going to jail, I had started attending church and I gave myself to God. I joined a non-denominational church and allowed the pastor of the church to become the vessel that God used to do his work, his signs, miracles, and wonders unto me, and I have allowed God to use me for His will and purpose. Romans 8:28, "and we know that all things work together for good to them that love God, to them who are called according to his purpose."

You can say I am in recovery! I am recovering from life's snags and potholes, but I didn't do it alone. I did it with the help from God. Jails, institutions and death ... this is what you hear in the halls of AA and NA. Yes, I have been there too, and done all of that! Been to jail, had a nervous breakdown, committed myself to an institution, and was dead—soul dead—before I found God. My experiences have helped me help many other people who may be suffering from homelessness, addiction, grief and loss, PTSD, depression and anxiety because I have personally endured these same challenges, life experiences and mental health symptoms.

This was the turning point in my life. I had to learn more about myself and my SWOT—my strengths, weaknesses, opportunities and threats—but more importantly, I had to ask God to forgive me and worked on building a relationship with Him. I knew God was calling for me because

I heard him; I heard him in my soul. I heard him and I ignored him. It was during this very difficult time in my life when I heard God speak.

"I got you now."

It was during this hard time, locked up and jailed, that I finally stopped and responded.

"Okay, I hear you. Have your way Lord, I am done doing it my way." When I surrendered and gave my will and care over to God, I never looked back. In the Bible, The Lord's Prayer, Matthew 6:9-13 states, "Thy kingdom come, thy will be done, in earth as it is in heaven." That's all I remember hearing in my mind. God will have his way, and I am glad he chose me to do his will. I am grateful to be able to take my experience of being *broken open* to help others. It is a privilege to counsel God's people and help shed light where there is darkness and tell a person they are perfectly and wonderfully made by God, and that they must live, and there is a purpose for their life! There is a word from God in Psalm 139:14 that says, "I will praise thee; for I am fearfully, and wonderfully made: marvelous are thy works; and that my soul knoweth right well."

How do you help another person who has been *broken open*, or on the verge of self-destruction and ask them to live? Someone with suicidal thoughts and no hope for a good future? When I allowed the Holy Ghost to dwell inside my broken soul and do a good work inside me is when I started to heal. Philippians 1:6 says, "Being confident of this very thing, that he which hath begun a good work in you will perform it until the day of Jesus Christ."

When I started reading the Bible more, I began to understand God and gain some inner peace. I learned that God's purpose for me was greater than I expected for myself, and these life events and situations, whether good or bad, were working for God's will and purpose for my life. God has qualified me to do this soul mending work, and I now *lead from within* with God's guidance. From my pain to purpose.

Romans 8:29-31 says, "For whom he did foreknow, he also did predestinate to be conformed to the image of his Son, that he might be the firstborn among many brethren. Moreover, whom he did predestinate, them he also called: and whom he called, them he also justified: and whom he justified, them he also glorified. What shall we then say to these things? If God be for us, who can be against us?"

I had to change myself—my thoughts, my mind, my actions and environment. I wanted to become a new creature in Christ Jesus. Paul writes in Romans 12:1-2, "I beseech you therefore, brethren, by the mercies of God, that ye present your bodies a living sacrifice, holy acceptable unto God, which is your reasonable service. And be not conformed to this world: but be ye transformed by the renewing of your mind, that ye may prove what is that good, and acceptable, and perfect, will of God."

I have wandered in the wilderness for a long time. I have carried my cross on this journey and I have put my faith in God. I have allowed God to carry me, use me, and guide me, and it has not been easy to give up all control, but as Christians we know that "for we walk by faith, not by sight," 2 Corinthians 5:7.

I began to listen to God's voice, and I began to change. I started to think more positively about myself, and life started to change. I read more of the Bible, and learned more about my role as a child of God and what God's role was for me. He was my father and I loved him. I knew I was building a relationship with God and with the Holy Ghost because of the warmth I felt inside my soul. People would tell me I was glowing, and I would say it's the Holy Spirit that lives within me.

What am I going to do now?

Well … life as I knew it had changed. I had no job, no car, no income, no home, and limited skills because the only job I had for over fifteen years was working for the courts. How was I going to function and get a life again? These were the thoughts that were going through my mind. I was transferred to a pre-release program for women from jail and that is where I put my plan for my new life together. When I was released from the program, I was released on parole and then probation. The correctional system would not let me go home so I had to reside in a sober house—a transitional home for women. A wonderful woman owned a transitional home for women called Clean Slate, and this is where I lived for over one year. This was another turning point in my life. I never knew about transitional living communities—a place to live and get your life back in order if you worked the program. Also, during this time, I had applied to a program at the St. Francis House in downtown Boston, MA. St. Francis is a nonprofit program, and the building is a city within a city.

St. Francis has many programs in their facility. They have a housing program in their building, they provide free lunch and dinner for the homeless. The Boston Medical Center contracts with them to provide medical care for the homeless and to St. Francis' program clients. They have a used clothing store where people get decent used clothing for interviews. They also have a job training program called MAP, the Moving Ahead Program. This program was created to help people who were getting out of prison or from being homeless and needed life and educational skills to get back into the workforce and society. This program paid the participants rent to live in transitional homes while attending the MAP program. They provided city bus passes to get to and from the program, and they gave a weekly stipend of sixty dollars to help with living expenses. I absolutely loved the program model because the program allowed you to take care of yourself while gaining skills to become functional in society again.

I had the opportunity to interview the President and CEO of St. Francis and I asked her how she became the CEO of the company as part of my programming at MAP. I told her one day I wanted to become a CEO of a company, and she told me anything is possible if you stay focused on your dreams. This was another step on my journey. I am proud to say that I am a graduate of Class 100 of MAP. Thank you, St. Francis House and the staff of the Moving Ahead Program, for all you do to help people regain their self-dignity, self-respect and their lives back.

I then moved to another transitional living community because it was less structured, and I was able to live more freely. I was sitting on the edge of my bed when the Lord spoke to me again.

"You are to create a transitional community for women."

I was shocked! There I was trying to get my life back in order while living in a transitional community myself and God says that he wants me to create a transitional home for women. I said to Him,

"I don't know what to do, and how will I do this?" I asked.

"I will give you everything you need."

Jeremiah 29:11, "For I know the plans I have for you," declares the Lord, "plans to prosper you and not to harm you, plans to give you hope and a future."

I later returned to Cambridge College and obtained my second master's degree in Mental Health and Addiction. I worked for a mental health agency as a community support worker. My job was to help people like me who had lost everything and were trying to regain their life back again. I still had no car or license because of the OUIs and was on foot, traveling several miles a day to work and to school on buses and trains. I know this is not unusual, but for me it was a drastic life change. But I knew that God makes a way out of no way. God is a way maker! "Trust in the Lord with all your heart and lean not on your own understanding; in all your ways submit to him, and he will make your paths straight," Proverbs 3:5-6.

While still working for the mental health clinic as a community support worker, I was promoted to clinician and became a mental health therapist. I was an independent contractor for the clinic, so I decided to create a business and I named it Soulful Essentials Inc. I became President and CEO of my own company, a counseling and wellness practice where I provide counseling and wellness services to this day.

Remember when God asked me to create a transitional community? In August 2011, I created a 501(c) 3, nonprofit called The Comfort Zone, Inc. The Comfort Zone will be a transitional home for women suffering from mental health and addiction issues. It has taken me time to get it up and running because of other life events, but when God asked me to create this program, I know it will be right on time.

I graduated with my Master of Education degree, with a concentration in Mental Health and Addiction and began this journey as a healer. I rented an office space and opened my counseling practice, Soulful Essentials Inc. This journey has been challenging and rewarding at the same time. God has provided and supplied me with all my needs. "And my God will meet all your needs according to the riches of His glory in Christ Jesus," Philippians 4:19.

My mental health and wellness practice is strong. I'm presently working on my Ph.D. for Integrative Medicine. I enjoy helping people who have endured the potholes and snags of life by providing counseling and assisting them in getting their lives back on track. I have personally endured my own mental health challenges and have learned that mental health runs in the family. I have taken medication during my lifetime to help regulate my mood, thoughts, feelings and emotions. I have worked with other healers to help guide me on my life's journey by allowing them to speak life back into me, and it has been a pleasure to assist others on working on becoming the best version of themselves after being *broken open.*

I hope that I show the same gift of empathy, compassion, and respect for humanity when I help people who are in need the same way it was given to me over fifty years ago by my God sent parents who adopted me and gave me a life. To God be the glory!

··· ABOUT VENITA QUALLS

Venita is an esteemed mental health and addition counselor, holding licensure in both Massachusetts and Georgia, where she has dedicated her career to supporting individuals grappling with a range of psychological challenges, including PTSD, addition, depression, anxiety, personality disorders and various other mental health conditions. As the visionary founder of Soulful Essentials Inc., Venita has created a sanctuary for healing and personal growth, drawing upon her extensive education and diverse therapeutic modalities to offer comprehensive care.

Her academic journey is marked by notable achievements, including two master's degrees, one in Education with a focus on Mental Health and Addiction Counseling, and the other in Management with a specialization in Nonprofit Management. These academic pursuits have equipped her with a unique blend of skills, enabling her to navigate both the clinical and administrative aspects of mental health care with equal proficiency. Currently, Venita is expanding her expertise through a Ph.D. program in Integrative Medicine, reflecting her commitment to holistic healing practices. She's not only well-versed in traditional counseling techniques but also trained in advanced somatic therapies like Brainspotting, Eye Movement Desensitization and Reprocessing (EMDR), Internal Family Systems (IFS), and is a certified Usui Reiki Master.

Email: *www.soulfulessentials@gmail.com*
LinkedIn: *https://www.linkedin.com/in/venita-chaney-qualls-5541a529*

20 ··· DIMINUENDO TO CRESCENDO

by Marcia Sears

I was born in Billings, Montana in the mid-fifties. Living in the country growing up, I was fortunate to have had many wonderful adventures. Like the time my beloved dog, Lady, and I made it down to the Yellowstone River for a picnic that I had packed in a knapsack for us. My mother only knew I was with my dog and knew Lady would bring me home. I also remember hunting pheasant with my dad, fishing with my Grampa and more. My imagination and curiosity led me on many adventures, and still do. As a family we would all go on Sunday drives in the blue Ford station wagon which opened my eyes to how other people lived and the beauty of nature.

My family moved from Montana to Washington state in the mid-sixties. Leaving behind my familiar home state and venturing westward into the unknown would test my resilience and strength. My dad had converted a school bus to a camper/moving van and we filled it with our personal treasures and headed west. The blue Ford station wagon was filled with half of the kids and snacks. I stayed with my mother on that long trip in that station wagon, following my dad and older sisters. Lady was with us, she lived until she was nearly nineteen.

The ensuing years were filled with challenges and hardships that would test my resilience and strength. I assumed the role of caregiver for our family as my parents worked to support us. Taking on the responsibility of cooking for a family of seven at age ten, on a very limited budget, gave me the "make something from nothing attitude" that I am grateful for. I learned the art of selflessness and sacrifice at a young age. The kitchen became my sanctuary; a place where I honed my skills and nurtured my loved ones with warmth and sustenance. Taking care of my baby brothers helped me with my babysitting career as the neighborhood parents used my talents. My older sisters were old enough to pursue other interests and I became Mother Marcia; a nickname that would be used throughout my life. Through the turbulent times and the weight of responsibility on my shoulders, I discovered a sense of purpose that would shape my path towards adulthood.

Of course, time is fleeting, and when I graduated from high school, I knew that more schooling wasn't my passion. The next best thing was cosmetology school, and although I loved it and my experience, I found myself reacting negatively to the products used. However, I still finished two thousand hours of schooling to pass the state board exam and am still licensed today.

I went on to work for a temp agency, and while my office skills were exemplary, I found myself daydreaming about traveling and adventure. As luck would have it, I heard about a job working on the railroad. I applied and then called every day until I got an interview. I'll never forget that interview. I was interviewed by both a woman and a man, and was told they were looking for top notched women. I stuck my chest out and declared that "I was a top notched woman!" Well, I got the job and they became my mentors.

I was one of the pioneering women who broke barriers by becoming a Sleeping Car Porter, a role traditionally held by Black men. I became a member of the brotherhood of the Sleeping Car Porters Union, which is now defunct. Women were new to this role and certainly not readily accepted by the men who were in charge of the operation of the train, i.e. conductors, brakemen etc. My journey as a trailblazer on the railroad paved the way for future generations of women to pursue roles in the transportation industry. I was often the only female employee on a train from Seattle to Chicago, and the only white onboard service employee at that time. This unique experience allowed me to gain a deeper understanding of diversity and inclusivity in the workplace. I embraced the opportunity to learn about different backgrounds and cultures, fostering a sense of unity and respect among us. I truly loved the many porters, waiters, cooks and dining car stewards who took me under their wing to teach me the ropes and help me succeed, without sacrificing my identity. Without Big John, Mr. T., Soup Maker, Ironhead, Mr. Carter and many more wonderful characters, I would not have had the long career I enjoyed.

The freight railroads were getting out of the passenger business and this is how Amtrak was started in 1974. I worked every freight railroad's particular sleeping cars, dome sleepers, all bedroom cars, ten and sixes, (ten roomettes, six bedrooms) and no two cars were alike. I served meals, shined shoes, made so many beds, and answered call bells at all hours of the night and day. Most importantly, I ensured our passengers loved their trips and didn't miss their stops!

I went on to work as a chair car attendant, waiter, bartender and even a second cook until becoming an Onboard Service Chief in 1988. Every job was based on seniority; on the railroad, seniority ruled. I had moved to southern California in 1983 when our crew base was closed in Seattle. I worked out of the most beautiful, Los Angeles Union Passenger Terminal from 1983-1993, when I was able to use my seniority to get back to Seattle, which had since reopened. I didn't return alone though; I had a beautiful baby girl in tow who was almost two years old. My family was in Seattle, and I wanted to raise my daughter in the northwest. We traveled from California in a twenty-four foot moving truck, towing my car. Being a single mother and traveling for work was a challenge that I somehow managed, but not without guilt and many, many tears.

My seniority enabled me to work the Coast Starlight to Los Angeles, four days on and six days off which helped me tremendously with childcare. When my daughter was thirteen, I was sidelined with an old back injury, and I thought I had given up my railroad career. I received a medical stipend from Amtrak and became an entrepreneur to make ends meet. I really had to rely on my willingness to do whatever it took to survive and prosper. After nearly five years, I was healed enough to want to finish my career with Amtrak to ensure I had the months required to retire with a full pension. The road back was not easy, and I was thwarted by management at every turn until I paid for a dexterity test to prove that I was able to work. Not everyone in management was fair and honest. I always was, and I would stand up for the employees in my charge. As a single working mother dedicated to raising and providing for my only child, I embraced the role of caregiver, provider and nurturer with unwavering commitment and love. Balancing the demands of work and parenthood presented its own set of challenges and rewards shaping me into a strong and resilient woman. I learned the true meaning of sacrifice, perseverance and unconditional love. My daughter was my reason for never giving up.

To all the women hired after me, I am proud to have helped pave the way and to those women that I was privileged to work with and become great friends with, I thank you from the bottom of my heart. It takes a village, and you were mine. I will always be proud of my life as a Railroader.

One thing I know in my heart of hearts is that we need to get back to each other. Humans need connection, and especially women. My journey to find my life's purpose really began with my first opportunity in network marketing. I was on a holistic path and looking for better products for my young daughter. Our sensitivity to caustic products was my driving force. I passed on many companies, as the products offered were not what I was looking for. My innate common sense and intuition has served me well as an entrepreneur. I knew that seeking training was important to not only understand what it meant to become a successful entrepreneur, but to become a better person too. Finding heart-centered people with the business acumen I wanted to learn, came from being a vendor, reading recommended self-development books and attending many, many seminars, retreats and network marketing groups. I am forever grateful to and for the many women that gave their knowledge and expertise freely with kindness.

I have met the most extraordinary women who have become my good friends through the toughest of times. Being open to holistic healing and forward thinking has helped me in more ways than I can name. These healers have brought out the very best in me and changed my very being. There was a time when my self-talk was not good, and depression had a deep grip on me. I couldn't parent my daughter the way she deserved, so I sought help through the railroad to find relief. I was so lucky to find a wonderful psychiatrist who turned out to also be the only woman in her class, many years prior. She helped me in those early years start to unravel the many layers of Marcia. She certainly changed the trajectory of my life. We knew that we had come to the end of our sessions together when we were exchanging recipes and just chit chatting. I adored her and will never forget her.

One thing is for sure, my self-preservation instincts are strong and my independence is nonnegotiable. I saw my mother juggling three or more jobs at once to take care of us, while my father jumped from one job to another. It's important that women have their own money and means to take care of themselves, which is something we have only been able to do since the mid-seventies, when women finally allowed to open a bank account and have a credit card in their own name. These life lessons have been instilled in my daughter; I have encouraged her to be a critical thinker and aware of who she spends her time and energy on. I was the mom who *wanted* her to talk to strangers. Learning body language, other people's energy, and how to make eye contact was important to discern who was safe and who was not.

My journey to self-love has taken many turns, with the loss of friends and loved ones. I am still learning to cope with grief by reaching out for help, which has evolved to pursuing hypnotherapy and taking spiritual classes. Growing up, I used humor to cope with pain and sadness. I could entertain myself for hours. Now, if I can make someone laugh, I am happy. We are stronger than we think and sometimes we have to laugh! I am always on the verge of laughter.

I wish I knew where my resilience and energy to love life full on came from. My belief is that everything is exactly the way it is supposed to be, in this moment. No longer caring what people think, and allowing myself to show up when I want, has been the greatest gift. My energy is special and unique, and while I give of myself freely and lovingly, I am in the crone stage of life where I have earned the very freedom I have longed for in my relationships to discern where and when I give my energy. This is a time of introspection and profound wisdom. These years are not a diminuendo, but a crescendo of knowledge—a culmination of lessons learned and experiences cherished. I stand as a testament to the beauty of aging, a bearer of insights that only time can bestow. I offer my wisdom as a beacon to those navigating the complexities of life. I speak of resilience, of the courage to pursue a path less trodden, and the grace to embrace change. My message is one of empowerment; encouraging each soul to find harmony in health and beauty, to live authentically, and to cherish every moment. Some say to go with the flow, but I have discovered a space above the flow where I just glide. Gliding is my all-knowing. I am magical and deserve all the universe has to offer. You do, too. We are *all* worthy of love.

My amazing life has been one of discovery, of finding beauty in nature and the importance of nurturing our bodies and the environment with toxin-free choices. I have embraced the role of mentor; eager to share the wealth of understanding I have learned throughout my lifetime. As I reflect on the chapters that have composed my story, I am filled with love and gratitude for the tapestry woven from threads of challenge and triumph. In my crone years, I am called on to pass on the legacy of my insights—to light the way for others. May my words be a guiding star, illuminating the path for you to a life lived with purpose, passion and peace.

··· ABOUT MARCIA SEARS

Marcia E. Sears stands as a beacon of inspiration in the realms of health, beauty and women's empowerment. With a passionate heart and entrepreneurial spirit, she has carved a niche for herself as a social biz entrepreneur and market builder, championing the cause of vegan and toxin-free products that cater to hair, skin and overall wellness. Her commitment is deeply rooted in the belief that everyone deserves access to pure, beneficial care that not only nurtures the body but also safeguards the environment. Her engagement with Spring Aqua Water Filtration and her expertise as a Licensed Cosmetologist are testaments to her dedication to promoting practices and products that embody her principles of health and sustainability. Beyond her business endeavors, Marcia is a fervent advocate for women's rights and empowerment. She leverages her platform and voice to support initiatives aimed at uplifting women, ensuring they have the opportunities to thrive in both personal and professional settings.

Website: *marciasears.mymonat.com*
Website: *https://springaqua.info/marciasears*
Website: *https://myainow.site?af=MarciaSears*

21 ··· ALL IN

by Tammy Cannon

It was my first birthday after losing my mom to the "c" word when she was only fifty-eight years old. As I rang in my fortieth birthday, I sat in a brown faux leather cushiony booth, mixing cream into my coffee in a classic white porcelain coffee mug. I was meeting a family member for a birthday breakfast, but our conversation turned out to be anything but celebratory. After this family member arrived and we settled in with greetings and placed our order, I was told something that shifted the trajectory of my life.

I was told that when family members learned of my young unmarried nineteen-year-old parents being pregnant with me, dark clouds of opinion rolled in and certain family members had suggested nipping the small babe in the bud, before it could blossom.

My breath was sucked right out of my chest, hearing this out-of-the-blue information. It was as if the clinking sound of cutlery throughout the cafe stopped at once—a collective holding of breath. I was unprepared emotionally for this news on a dual milestone birthday, turning forty and it being the first of forever birthdays that my mom wouldn't be calling to wish a "happy birthday."

Intellectually, I now understand that this was the climate of the times for my interracial family in the seventies. My parents' choice to have their child blossom and bloom was a testimony to their love for each other, and for me. As confusing and challenging as it was to hear, on that particular day, it allowed me to turn the handle and crack open—ever so slightly—the floodgates of grief that I'd tamped down since my mom's passing. It's been almost ten years now and I've spent the last decade grieving, learning and diving deep into old wounds to break some well-worn patterns that I didn't even know existed in my subconscious. And so, my story is about breaking patterns of self-sabotage from old wounds and hurts, to invite you to pull into your heart the golden nuggets of self-reliance, resiliency, and living into the power of what's possible for your life. Are you ready? Let's begin.

I had already known that I was created out of wedlock. I was eleven when my parents decided to add onto our home—a big great room with a bar, guest bath, fireplace with brick hearth and surround, and a pool. The bar was nearly finished, and pictures and other memorabilia were behind the bar awaiting their place on the wall. I had picked up a stack of items, and there it was. A picture of my parents on their wedding day. My mother's baby bump would be ... I had counted on my fingers ... five months along. It occurred to me then that I had never seen a photo of their wedding day before then. And in that moment, the first seed of unworthiness was planted. My young brain said to itself, "you were an accident." So many versions of that thought have created an unworthiness pattern in my brain—a pattern that I have subconsciously rehearsed in one way or another throughout my life. The news on my fortieth birthday was just the key I needed to open the door and examine my life. It was a gift that has just taken me a while to fully unwrap.

I had an amazing childhood; I was loved all around and still am. Of course, there were the normal pockmarks we all experience, but by and large, I look back fondly. But I do see the early pattern of "here you go," and "there it goes," that had emerged in my memories. In other words, "you're not worthy of this." One of my earliest memories of this was in preschool. A teacher's aide gave me a piece of gum and told me not to tell anyone where I got it. But I'm not supposed to lie, right? So, when another child asked me where I got it, what do you think I said? The teacher's aide then came up to me with a reprimand and said I'd never get a piece of gum again.

"Here you go ... There it goes."

I now see how wrong she was, but my preschool self was confused and hurt. In examining these mini memories, another pattern emerged. Self-reliance. As an only child, I had to encounter life alone.

First day of school.

Family stress.

Groping by adolescent boys.

An adult who asks you to lie about gum.

Alone. No siblings to share the excitement or the humiliation of the day with. But inside, I was strengthening my inner reliance. There was no other option except to feel sorry for myself, and I didn't want to dwell there. I had to give myself my own advice and keep going. When I look back at myself from birth to fourteen, that girl was so strong. And now, at forty-nine, I'm channeling her strength and thanking her for building those muscles.

Who do *you* rely on when the highs are high, or the lows are low? Have you cultivated an inner reliance to carry you through? Your reliance on yourself is related to your intuition as well. Strengthening these muscles will propel you forward in your life and business. It will help you see that you have everything you need to have everything you want. Read that again.

It all begins and ends with you having your own back.

I encourage you to examine where you are relying on yourself and where you'd like to improve. You may find that you are stronger than you think, and you are so worthy of that strength and using it to build your empire. After that birthday breakfast, I got in the car and called my husband while shedding a few tears. But I didn't stay in the sadness of what I'd heard. It didn't interrupt my relationship with that family member, either. Two things were happening, though, as I look back. One, another muscle emerged: resiliency. Think of resiliency as buoyancy, or a bouncing back quickly after an event. And two, what I didn't know was that by not addressing what I'd heard and processing it with loving awareness, I added it to the strings of unworthiness in my subconscious and it was affecting other areas of my life. There were goals I just couldn't reach. There was behavior I wasn't proud of.

It wasn't until I went back through events in my life to discover the patterns of self-sabotage. I hadn't done the work to sit in those circumstances and create some new perspectives around them. So, while resiliency is such a great skill, combining it with new awareness can interrupt some of those patterns. Combing through my memories, another painful time emerges. I was working in the marketing department at our county's healthcare institute. Part of my job was to talk with the hospital administrator and write his newsletter to all the employees and staff. But he didn't like my voice.

As I approached the end of my ninety-day employee trial, he denied permanent employment until I took voice lessons. I remember being so devastated and crying before going to work. It kicked off a dark couple of months for me until I eventually quit. I didn't have the resiliency and self-reliance at twenty-six years old like I do now. I could have sued! Basing my employment on a character determination and causing duress was grounds for a lawsuit. This would not have been the course of action I'd have taken all those years ago, but thinking about that circumstance in a more empowered way would have allowed me to stay confident and fall into a dark place. Like all these other circumstances, I added it to that well-worn path of unworthiness. "Here's a job for you, Tammy. Oops, there it goes." And I didn't think about it again until I started to work on myself. Wild.

The takeaway here is: don't dwell in the feelings that present themselves when things happen, instead, process them with loving thoughts about yourself. In my coaching business, we use powerful techniques to explore new perspectives and gain better awareness about ourselves and what we're creating in our lives. It can be painful to open to past hurts, which is why most of us ignore and tamp down the uncomfortable things of life. But the reward is so much greater than the hurt when you do this work. You'll find the richness of forgiveness for yourself and others. You can move toward what you want in your life versus staying stuck in judgment of circumstances and other people.

The first time this clicked for me, I had just finished teaching on a webinar and a family member came in and said something that would have normally sent me on a spiral of insecurity and hurt. But something miraculous happened because I did the work on managing my mind. Do you know what happened? Nothing.

I didn't respond like I would have in the past. I didn't pick a fight. I didn't make it mean anything about me even though the comment was directed at me and about me. Instead, I had compassion for this person and thought that perhaps he was projecting to make himself feel better. Maybe he'd had a bad day and I was a safe place to be flippant. All the hard work I had been doing suddenly clicked, right then and there … in the heat of the moment. That little nugget of change is what sparked me to become a certified life coach. The work *works*.

The only thing we can control in this world is ourselves. Period. And this is good news! It means we alone have the power to change the narrative in our lives. This is what I love the most out of everything that comes out of the healing process, because all the possibilities for my life become right there for the taking. In examining my patterns of unworthiness, I could literally see the strings of so many circumstances that were keeping me stuck and holding me back. They showed up as strings of thoughts in my mind without my knowing it.

The most dominant thought was "this isn't working." Whether it was my latest launch, an Instagram live that no one attended, not working out consistently or underearning. These were all variations of the same thought, and by looking a little closer at the pattern of thought, I was able to decipher it. *"This* isn't working" meant *"I* wasn't working," which ultimately meant *"I* wasn't worthy of *this."*

I couldn't meet the possibilities in. my life. I blocked them from coming to fruition, which eventually led me on a journey through the past to uncover and examine those threads of unworthiness. So many memories emerged, and I examined them to learn the lessons in them. And so, I let go. I cut the strings and reshaped my relationship with those circumstances, gave myself a big hug, and began to focus on what I do wanted and not on what I didn't want.

Our brain is hardwired for impending death. It thinks it's keeping us safe from bears and wild berries, like in the caveman days. It also looks for and focuses on the negative things in life, which keeps us from experiencing the richness of possibility our lives have to offer. Stepping out of the cave today looks like: starting to date again, building a bigger business, going to the gym, stepping on the scale. Our brain thinks these things are dangerous, so it says, "you'll never meet the right person, so just stay home." It says, "you've never done it before, so let's keep our business at status quo." It says, "your clothes are wrinkled, so don't go to the gym, stay home on the couch." And it says, "uh-oh you've gained some weight, let's go have a snack."

But when we live an intentional life we can start to question what our brain is telling us and move forward in your life. When we lean into what's possible for us, those garden-variety thoughts seem to dissipate. Now I tell my brain now, "I'm doing it anyway," and it eliminates decision fatigue by going after something I really want. It also breeds commitment to myself and my goals. For many of my clients and in examining myself, decision and commitment are two of the most important aspects to living a life on purpose.

Think about a goal *you* want to achieve and ask yourself if you've truly decided to go after it. If not, you won't feel that determination and commitment.

It's at this intersection of strategy and implementation where most of us get stuck. As an entrepreneur, it looks like this: you've created a vision board for your business and the most beautiful pictures have been cut out of magazines and glued onto it. You're filled with so much possibility and excitement for what could be, but then you strategize and figure out what it's going to take to bring your vision to reality. How are you going to get there and what tools will you need? Then you create a plan and get all those actions on your calendar.

"Go live on Instagram on Tuesday at 2pm."

But then ... your brain decides to do something funny. When it's Tuesday at 2pm and time to go live, your brain might say, "Oh, girl. You slept heavily last night and your eyes are puffy. Let's go live another time. So, even though you have this beautiful vision and thorough strategy and specifics on your calendar, you don't cross the intersection of implementation.

This also happens when you create a vision of what your body will look like on vacation in a few months. You decide on a strategy to make it a reality. You then add intermittent fasting, Crossfit, yoga, clean eating, and mono meals to your calendar.

"Cardio on Mondays, Wednesdays and Fridays at 4pm."

"Portioned eating seven nights a week."

In theory, it seems feasible ... until you have an exhausting day and when it's time to go to the gym your brain says, "Nah, honey. We're exhausted, let's stay in."

It's at this intersection that we're missing true decisiveness and commitment toward our goal of looking like a goddess on vacation. When there is another option that requires less of us, our brain will offer it to us—every time. But when we eliminate all the other decisions, which present as excuses in our brain, life opens up for us.

You'll know you're in commitment when there is zero mind drama around what you want to do. Think of a commitment you've made— marriage, a degree, a certification, giving birth. It's that feeling of going all in and not entertaining any other options. Eliminating decision fatigue is what helped me to become five pounds stronger in ninety days. I shocked even myself when I committed to working out six days a week. I had never done that before. But I eliminated all other options and leaned into the possibility that not only could I change my body, but I could strengthen my brain muscles too. And that's no joke. When you practice new thoughts, you strengthen brain muscles by creating new neural pathways that reshape your beliefs. And these new beliefs become your new baseline. You become a person who believes in herself and live with intention. You *can* have it all, you're just one thought away.

When was the last time you leaned into possibility? Have you stopped dreaming and visioning? Are you stuck at the intersection of strategy and implementation?

After doing the work on becoming five pounds stronger, I applied the same mental process to putting in an English cutting garden. After that, I tackled my primary bedroom closet. When you can train your mind to focus on what you want—instead of what you don't want—ideas, circumstances, abundance, coincidences, and people flow to you easily. Society conditions us to focus on what we don't want, and what we don't have. It's time to dream again about what is possible in our lives.

So, dear reader, I pose these questions to you now. What *is* possible for your life? Can you look within and find the worthiness to go after it?

I can tell you that you *are* worth it.

When I finally stopped to examine those well-worn patterns of thinking, there were some painful memories that appeared, but the joy in cutting them loose and creating new perspectives for myself was so worth the effort to go "there." I don't know what your life looks like in the past or how certain ways of thinking have shaped your life, but I invite you to get to know yourself a little bit better.

Go there with her.

You are worthy.

⸱⸱⸱ ABOUT TAMMY CANNON

Tammy is a highly empathetic and compassionate coach with a diverse background that enables her to connect with people from all walks of life. Her coaching style creates a safe and nurturing environment where individuals feel comfortable sharing their experiences and challenges. Tammy has a unique ability to make others feel at ease, often leaving them with a sense of relaxation akin to a spa experience. As a coach, Tammy specializes in supporting real estate professionals in finding greater happiness and meaning in their lives. Drawing from her own experience as a licensed realtor, she understands the unique challenges and demands that agents face on a baily basis. She also enjoys renovating homes, combing her passion for design and real estate.

Tammy splits her time between Washington state and Arizona, immersing herself in the diverse landscapes and communities of both regions. In her free time, Tammy can be found tending to her garden, finding solace and joy in nature's beauty. With her warm and caring approach, she is dedicated to helping others live their best lives and achieve their goals.

Free Agent's Blueprint on How to Feel Amazing for more and better listings:
https://www.tammycannon.com/amazing
Follow me on Instagram - *https://www.instagram.com/thetammycannon*
Email: *Tammy@tammycannon.com*

··· ABOUT E.P. HOUSE

E.P. House, led by founder and CEO Kristin Bentley, is a boutique publishing house that provides mentorship to global changemakers. With an unwavering commitment to quality and a keen eye for talent, E.P. House has soared to unprecedented heights. Every author has achieved bestselling status and international recognition, earning prestigious awards. With a steadfast dedication to excellence, E.P. House continues to push the boundaries of traditional publishing, amplifying the voices of those who dare to make a difference.

Milton Keynes UK
Ingram Content Group UK Ltd.
UKHW042205070524
442338UK00005B/213